DESIGN
PRESENTATIONS
FOR ARCHITECTS

DESIGN PRESENTATIONS FOR ARCHITECTS

Michael Iver Wahl, AIA

VNR Van Nostrand Reinhold Company
_____New York

Copyright © 1987 by Van Nostrand Reinhold Company Inc.
Library of Congress Catalog Card Number 86-28291
ISBN 0-442-29150-7

Printed in the United States of America
Designed by Azuretec Graphics

Van Nostrand Reinhold Company Inc.
115 Fifth Avenue
New York, New York 10003

Van Nostrand Reinhold Company Limited
Molly Millars Lane
Wokingham, Berkshire RG11 2PY, England

Van Nostrand Reinhold
480 La Trobe Street
Melbourne, Victoria 3000, Australia

Macmillan of Canada
Division of Canada Publishing Corporation
164 Commander Boulevard
Agincourt, Ontario M1S 3C7, Canada

16 15 14 13 12 11 10 9 8 7 6 5 4 3 2

Library of Congress Cataloging-in-Publication Data
Wahl, Michael, 1943–
    Design presentations for architects.

    Includes index.
    1. Architecture—Designs and Plans—Presentation drawings.   I. Title.
NA2714.W34   1987   720'.28'4   86-28291
ISBN 0-442-29150-7

CONTENTS

	Preface	vii
	Acknowledgments	viii
1.	Why Clients Respond	1
2.	Drawing Skills Review	5
3.	Languages and Phases	15
4.	Composition	29
5.	Projections	45
6.	Entourage	61
7.	Media	73
8.	Exhibits	89
9.	Presentation	93
10.	Ethics	101
11.	Drawing and Rendering Samples	103
	Bibliography	131
	Index	133

PREFACE

A successful presentation enables a client to understand, like, and decide to build a project. Failing this, a successful presentation should at least allow the client to state his objections clearly. A successful presentation is a brilliantly conceived plan that is skillfully developed and sensitively executed. A successful presentation is an all-out effort for a single word: *yes*. Anything less is inadequate. Everything more is a waste. *Yes* is the most important word in design.

Graphics is only a part of a successful presentation, and it is only a part of this book. Presentation is as much about people as it is about your design solution. It is about you personally. It concerns what you say and how you say it. It is also about your client as a human being and what makes him respond. Advertising agencies, salesmen, psychologists, commercial display designers—even circus clowns—possess knowledge that we can use to make successful presentations. In addition to the tips and books mentioned in the text, the bibliography at the back of this book recommends numerous volumes that can help you develop your presentation skills.

This book does not offer a wide variety of approaches to design presentation. In fact, it provides only one—but it is an easy one to learn. A broad variety of examples of different rendering approaches has been included in chapter 12 to give you an idea of the range of options available.

ACKNOWLEDGMENTS

In addition to the individual recognition given elsewhere to those who generously allowed their work to be published in this book, I would like to express my appreciation to the following individuals, without whom this book would not have been produced: Lisa Portwood; Kol Wahl; Jim Kudrna; Nick Harm; Brad Black; Dan Lare, ASLA; Ray Yeh, AIA; Ron Hess, AIA; Ross Bell, AIA; William Muchow, FAIA; Robert Engelke, AIA; Ed Warner; Skay McCall; Burt Welz; Jim Yeatts; and Richard Austin, ASLA.

A special thanks to the students who have contributed to this work and to the fullness of my life.

WHY 1
CLIENTS
RESPOND

Clients begin to respond to you when they first contact you—with that first phone call or in that first meeting. Your presentation begins with your receptionist, your office, and your first actions.

Your client begins to say *yes* each time you listen rather than talk during your first meeting, when you carefully take notes on all that he says. These actions show that you want to learn about your client. Information is one of the critical chips in the game of negotiating. Start collecting those chips early in your first conference.

INFORMATION YOU NEED

The information you need concerns not only the client's project, but the client himself. It is tempting to rely on elaborate logic and mountains of data. But in the game of persuasion, emotions are equally powerful. Examine the complexity of your client.

First, he or she has *instincts* and will act on them. If you stand near the edge of a high place, you may feel an instinctual response. These "gut feelings" are present from birth. Often, the harder a client is pressed, the more his or her instincts will surface.

In addition, your client's response will be based on *learned behavior.* These are actions that stem from experience. The first time you touched a hot stove, you learned never to do it again. Learned behavior includes your client's usual methods of operation and negotiation. *Attitudes,* also based on our life experiences, are one type of learned behavior. They are the viewpoints from which we habitually operate.

Finally, all people have needs that, in turn, inspire buying motives:

- recognition and superiority
- health and long life

- comfort
- appetizing food and drink
- security
- money
- protection of one's family
- approval of opposite sex
- minimal labor
- amusement
- information and education
- dependability
- curiosity
- possession

Your client's individual needs and motives suggest the type of appeal you should make. Explain how your solution will make the client:

- feel more important
- feel happier
- be more comfortable
- be more prosperous
- have less or easier work
- have more security
- be more attractive
- be better liked
- have some unique distinction
- have, improve, or maintain health
- get a bargain

The presentation plan is based on this process.

To make a successful presentation you must learn about your client's instincts, experiences, needs and motives. Most designers conscientiously research the functional problem and the spatial needs of their clients. Some even ask their favorite color and if they want anything special in the project. But you need to know more (fig. 1-1). Get to know your clients, not just what they want to build.

Personal information about clients can be easily gained in several ways. All business meetings are accompanied by small talk. Although these light conversations are usually intended only to fill time and reduce tension, they are often rich in personal information. People are usually quite willing to discuss themselves and their personal interests during these casual talks. Careful observation of a client's apparel, car, and personal effects can convey useful insight into the client as well.

Once you feel you know and understand your clients, you can create better designs for them. Now all you have to do is make a presentation that also satisfies those same needs and motives.

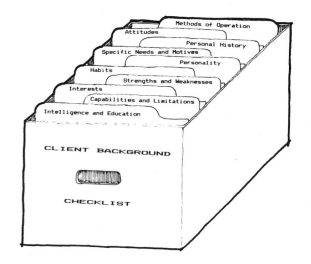

1-1. Form a systematic picture of your clients.

POSITIVE RESPONSES

Surprisingly, many architects don't know when to pin a client down to a positive response—to commit him to *yes*. Try for a trial closing on the issue:

- any time you think you can get it
- after strong points in your presentation
- after overcoming an obstacle presented by the client
- when your demonstration ends
- when your client shows signs of saying *yes*

Many also do not recognize when they are being told *yes*. Your client is saying yes if he or she:

- shows intense interest
- makes statements advancing the discussion (e.g., How long would this take?)
- shows a willingness to move into greater detail
- indicates objections are satisfied
- shows hesitation
- nods
- makes a favorable comment on some aspect of the project
- relinquishes the initiative in the discussion
- shifts the attack to simple questions and trivial issues
- allows himself to be moved even one small step toward commitment
- compliments you on the handling of even a small part of the project

NEGATIVE RESPONSES

Your client may say no because the project does not meet his or her needs. This means you did not do your homework—you did not learn enough about the client. But there are also other reasons for a negative response that are not directly related to the design.

Problems with You

An architect's grooming, clothing, grammar, conversation habits, nervous habits, posture, prejudices, rudeness, ego, temper, and carelessness should not be allowed to interfere with the acceptance of a good design. Idiosyncrasies of this type are luxuries that a good designer cannot afford.

Remember that a sense of humor is a two-edged sword. To have one is necessary, but a poor one can be worse than none. Make an obnoxious joke or laugh at the wrong thing and rapport is lost.

Introversion and shyness can also be unnecessary enemies. No one in the room knows any more about your design and its merits than you. The client expects you to succeed, or you would not have been hired. Do not be shy about sharing your enthusiasm for your work—your client wants to be as happy about it as you are.

Problems with the Client

Price, prejudice, power, and procrastination have been cited as common client-based reasons for rejecting a design. Anticipate probable objections and rehearse responses to these objections prior to beginning any final presentation.

The wrong style of appeal may also lead a client to hedge rather than to say yes. Even if you correctly identified your client's needs, your appeal might not be sufficiently forceful to demonstrate this.

If your client is acting as an agent for another, he or she may not have the authority to say yes. In addition, peer pressure can influence your client and deny the acceptance that you have earned. Part of knowing your clients involves understanding who influences them and who has final approval of your work. Learn both the formal and the informal approval procedures of your client so that you can convince the people that count.

Your client may have secret or hidden motives when hiring you. Careful negotiation during the presentation can expose and clarify these, but it is better to know about them beforehand. This can be difficult, since the client may be unaware of these motives himself. Some motives are sensitive, and the client may deliberately conceal them. If you discover one of these, the client will surely object to it being publically announced. Use it to your advantage but keep it to yourself. Motives are by their nature complex and difficult to separate, and they are hard to satisfy separately.

It is said that every man is three people: the man he thinks he is, the man others think he is, and the man he really is. A successful presentation will appeal to all three.

Recognizing a Negative Response

Most people cannot give an unqualified *no*. The motives behind the negative response may make saying *no* even more difficult. As a result most people use escape mechanisms and excuses. Do not be confused by this hedging, and do not ignore it. Watch for the following tactics:

Compensation substitutes another response for the desired response: "I am not happy with your design but your renderings are beautifully prepared."

Sublimation is the act of substituting a "good" action or emotion for a "bad" one.

Organizing paperwork after a disagreement is an example.

Regression is evident when a client or associate begins to act less than his age, experience, or position in an effort to avoid responsibility.

Rationalization consists of an elaborate web of justifications directed at avoiding action or responsibility.

Repression will often surface as memory failure; a person honestly cannot remember an unpleasant issue.

Identification begins subtly but terminates in an astonishing transformation. Before your eyes, a person will change his personality and become someone that he feels would be more adequate in this difficult situation. For example, someone you have come to like and respect starts talking exactly like John Wayne, Dad, or some other power figure.

When any of these behaviors starts to surface, give your client a little slack. He is evidently under a lot of stress. You need to find the cause, not press him to a defensive *no*.

Examples of how clients try to reject a design tactfully include:

The design isn't suitable.

Credit is too difficult right now.

We can't afford it.

I want to think it over.

I'm too busy right now.

Personal problems or ties won't allow me to do this.

I need to discuss this with others.

My boss, wife, etc., will never go for this.

We are okay the way we are now and really don't need these changes.

Unspoken negative reaction might be indicated by increased restlessness, loss of interest in the subject, changing of the subject, and prolonged silence. Learn to recognize negative response from the body language and facial expressions of your client (many good books on this are available).

Tactfully end a meeting that degenerates into a string of excuses and negative behaviors so that you can regroup. Following such a meeting, immediately review the events in detail. Determine exactly *when* the client started to resist the design. This is often the best clue available in fully understanding *why* the design was rejected.

DRAWING 2
SKILLS
REVIEW

Design presentation presumes the ability to draw. No graphic tricks are a substitute for it. Poor drawing ability suggests poor design ability to a client. Since most design presentations begin with a fine drawing, a moment should be given to a review of common techniques used in learning this critical skill.

TOOLS AND MATERIALS

Two separate sets of equipment and materials are recommended to improve drawing skills. The first will help you increase line control. The second set will help you add flamboyance and power to your drawings.

For set 1, buy a legal-size clipboard and a package of cheap typing paper. Computer paper or copy-machine paper are expensive but good substitutes. Do not buy erasable paper, as pencil and felt-tip markers smear badly on it. Do not bother with papers that have a "rag" content. They are not good for these drawings, though they are costly. Also buy ⅛-inch graph paper. Right now, you need only one sheet.

Now pick your pens. A Flair, a Sharpie, and a razor-point are best. Also buy a couple of #2 pencils with erasers. Finally buy a pink eraser—just for security; you will not be using it much.

Set up your clipboard as shown in figure 2-1, with one sheet of typing paper over the graph paper. The rest of the typing paper is used to pad the hard surface of the clipboard. With this arrangement you can draw straight freehand lines. Your vertical lines will be truly vertical, and your horizontal lines will be straight. More important, you will always have consistent guidelines for your lettering. Finally, you will always be thinking and drawing in scale. All of this leads to better control. The best part of this setup is that it is cheap and easily available. You can do reams of

drawings for pennies. This means more practice, and more practice means more confidence.

For set 2 buy a pad of cheap 18- by 24-inch newsprint paper at your nearest art-supply store. While you are there, pick up a package of vine charcoal. On this pad draw big, draw bold, draw fast. These materials are cheap, so be flamboyant. Charcoal will not allow you to get fussy with detail.

Both setups will teach you to draw line drawings. There are other types and methods, but line drawings are easier, so they will dominate this book.

GESTURE DRAWING

Gesture drawing is often used at the start of a life drawing session as a warm-up exercise. It teaches an artist to see the most important lines in an object. In gesture drawing the model quickly goes through a sequence of spontaneous, exaggerated poses. Each pose is held for only about five seconds. The artist must capture the essence of these poses with quick line drawings.

Often the longest lines of an object are the most important. A line might begin at the fingertips of the right hand and flow down continuously to the toes of the left foot. Gesture drawing encourages you to see these long lines. Forget names of body parts. Look only for long lines that, by themselves, describe a posture (fig. 2-2).

You say you have no model? No matter. Turn one way and sketch whatever you see for five seconds. Turn another way and do the same again. Repeat the process, facing in different directions, at least ten times. Warm up this way every time you draw. It takes under one minute.

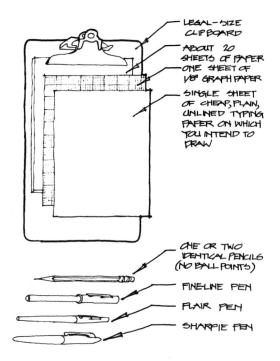

2-1. Tools and materials for drawing.

2-2. Gesture drawing.

You can use either your clipboard setup or the newsprint to make gesture drawings. Since you are trying to loosen up, work fast, work *big*.

SCUMBLING

Scumbling is another technique often used as a warm-up exercise. It also aids a designer in studying masses and voids in a composition without being distracted by details of the outline. Charcoal and newsprint are best for scumbling.

In scumbling the model usually shifts poses every fifteen seconds. You are not looking at lines, but studying the sizes and shapes of the masses and voids that you see (fig. 2-3). Do not look at your paper and guess. Look at the model and get the real proportions correct. Four of these drawings per work session will be enough to warm up.

Scumbling is not only a good exercise; it is a valuable tool that will help you with composition, discussed in chapter 4.

No model? Follow the same routine as for gesture drawing: face one way for fifteen seconds and draw, then turn in another direction and draw.

PROPORTIONAL DRAWING

Many people find that seeing the true proportions of a model, building, or other subject is difficult. Commonly, five students make the same drawing with five different sets of proportions. In art school it could be called interesting, individual, or creative. To an architect, it is inaccurate.

You should have no need to guess proportions when you can measure them. Hold your pencil vertical at arm's length and measure the overall height of the subject that you are drawing (fig. 2-4). Use the top of the pencil

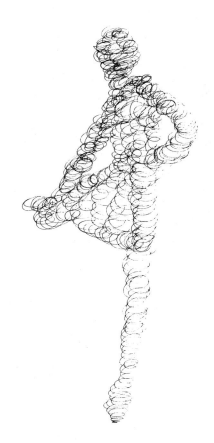

2-3. Scumbling.

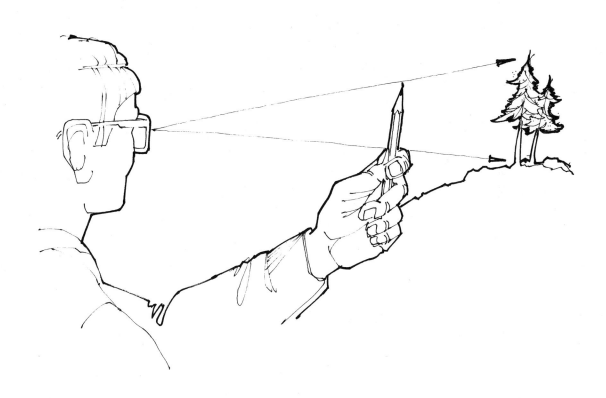

2-4. Proportional drawing.

and your thumb to scale this vertical dimension. Then place the pencil flat on your paper and transfer the dimension to the drawing surface. To accomplish this, quickly put a small tick mark on the paper where the top of the pencil falls and a second mark where your thumb falls. Now again hold the pencil at arm's length while you look at the subject of your drawing, but hold the pencil horizontal to scale the overall width of the building.

Transfer this dimension to your clipboard as before. Now make a visual judgment. Does the building look to be twice as tall as it is wide, for example? Use the graph paper (always under the sheet on which you are drawing) to verify the relationship. Rough in the outline of the building.

Now turn your attention to the secondary masses. Perhaps your building is divided into three wings. Scale each of these wings

(secondary masses) as before, and transfer the dimensions to your drawing. Subdivide the overall mass of the building accordingly. Finally, scale and place the details, such as windows and doors, within each wing, or secondary mass.

Scaling in this way is a good means for accurate sketching, and it will make you more conscious of true proportions in a composition.

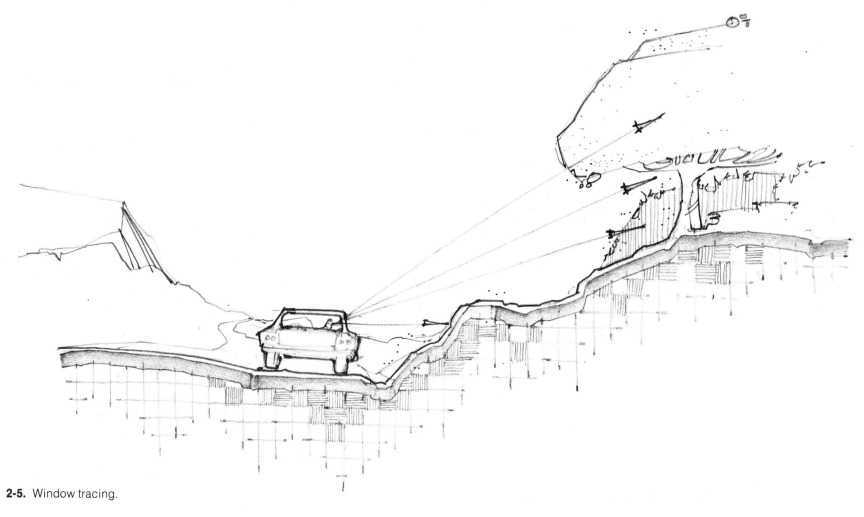

2-5. Window tracing.

WINDOW DRAWING

If you are just learning to draw and you have difficulty locating objects in their proper place in your drawings, try the following technique. Get into your car and take a drive. Take a grease pencil, some paper towels, and some window cleaner with you. When you find a scene worth drawing, park the car so that you can look at the scene through one of the side windows. Now trace the scene directly onto the window (fig. 2-5). This technique may not be very elegant, but it will give you practice in placing everything in the drawing in its proper place. A paper towel and window cleaner will put you back on the road searching for another worthy scene. After an afternoon of work, you will have clean windows and greatly increased drawing skill.

STRUCTURAL DRAWING

Structural drawing produces what are usually called stick figures (fig. 2-6). They are very helpful in life drawing if your model is in a complex pose. Structural drawing helps you to unravel complicated subjects with ease. Just replace major bones with single lines. Once you have these "sticks" in the right places, use the proportional drawing method to confirm each stick's length.

Other complex objects, such as trees, can also be more easily drawn by first using this technique to discover their underlying structure.

CUBIST DRAWING

Cubist drawing involves replacing real, complex forms with their closest geometric equivalent. The human head can be approximated by a circle or an ellipse. A nose is roughly a triangle. Reducing a composition to simple shapes allows you to study them without confusing detail (fig. 2-7). The proportion of each shape can be scaled using techniques previously discussed. Often these correctly scaled shapes are "hung" in their proper position on a "stick" skeleton.

Once the shapes are lightly sketched, a detailed drawing in darker pencil will be easy to create. Cubist drawing can also be used to study the shape scheme in a composition (see chapter 4).

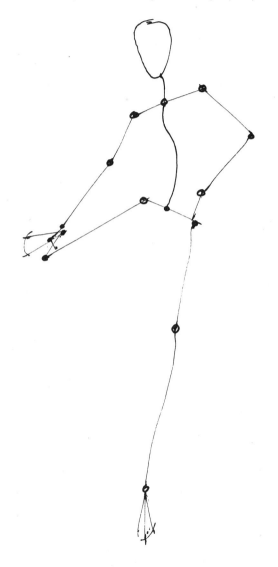

2-6. Structural drawing.

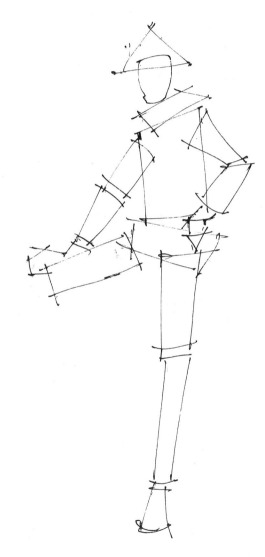

2-7. Cubist drawing.

CONTOUR LINE DRAWING

Each true line in a drawing has a unique character of its own. Whether it is an important line or not, it must be accurate—"true." The true lines are on the object or model you are drawing. Your goal is to transfer these lines from the model to your drawing. The line in the drawing must wiggle if the true line wiggles. It must bend if the true line bends.

The secret to making true lines in your drawing is to look at the subject, not at your paper. Try this. Get a good friend to sit very still, facing you. Put your clipboard and pencil in front of you and look at his or her face. Really study its details. Do the eyes slope up or down? In which direction does each small hair in the eyebrows run? Study the total face very carefully.

Now, without looking down at your clipboard, put your pencil on the paper and begin to draw. *Never* take your eyes off the face. *Never* lift the pencil from the paper. Draw the whole face with one long, continuous, expressive line. Pretend that you are not drawing, but actually touching the face with your pencil: you are a blind person running your hand over the face of a stranger. Exaggerate. If, for example, you see razor stubble, make a real field of stumps as your hand jolts and bumps over each whisker. Draw only what you see. Draw all that you see.

Now look down at the drawing for the first time. Of course it looks funny—but the truth is there. Although out of proportion, it really looks like your friend (fig. 2-8). If you had used the same technique but looked down once or twice and exaggerated a bit more, it would become caricature drawing.

MINIMAL DRAWING

Combining all the skills you have learned thus far, complete your best drawing. If you are drawing a person, use structural drawing to lightly sketch a stick figure. Proportionally measure the sticks. Very lightly hang the geometric shapes on the structure. Then use contour line drawing to carve the true lines onto the framework that you have constructed. Look down as little as possible during the contour line phase of the drawing.

Now take out an eraser. Begin removing everything possible from your drawing. If two eyes are not required to tell the story, erase one. If the drawing is understandable without a pocket, remove it. Get down to the absolute, uncompromised essense (fig. 2-9). Sometimes less really is more.

2-8. Contour line drawing.

2-9. Minimal drawing.

MEMORY DRAWING

Deciding which lines in a composition are most important can be difficult. If you can find them, they should be darkened and emphasized.

One technique used to identify important lines is memory drawing. Glance at a new subject for only an instant on first sight. Wheel around and draw all that you can remember. Pay attention to what you draw first, as it is probably the most important.

Memory drawing can also be used to draw scenes you saw in the past. I have not been to Monument Valley in Arizona for years, but figure 2-10 shows how I remember it. Note that such drawings lack detail, but they do tell something about the hierarchy of lines in a place and show what at least one human found to be of lasting importance.

PHOTO DRAWING

Photo drawing is just the opposite of memory drawing. If you try to draw a front loader or a road grader from memory, you will have trouble. Complex objects are too rich in detail to remember. Instead, look around for a photograph of the object you want to draw, and make a drawing based on the photograph (fig. 2-11).

There is no need to guess about details when you can know them. Many architects project a slide of a scene onto paper and then trace the image. No one is looking for fine art in your renderings; clients want, and pay for, good drawings. Whatever technique you use to make these drawings is perfectly acceptable.

2-11. Photo drawing.

2-10. Memory drawing.

LIFE DRAWING

Drawing from photographs is easy because living, three-dimensional, large moving objects are reduced to small, still, two-dimensional equivalents before you start. There is, however, no substitute for drawing from life. You can learn to draw *a* tree from a book. You learn about *trees* from life. In order to keep learning and growing in drawing skill, this activity is critical. Learn to draw skies from skies. Books can give you only a start. Life drawing will continue to be useful in your daily work. Moreover, some things will never look right if drawn from photos or memory. For example, never attempt to memory-draw drapes; the folds just will not look right. But if you have one piece of real cloth, you can simulate drapes and draw them perfectly (fig. 2-12).

THUMBNAIL SKETCHING

This rapid technique has several applications. Thumbnails are used to describe the general massing and appearance of a setting or object. Use any drawing style you like, but each sketch can be only one or two inches in any dimension. Unnecessary detail is automatically identified and omitted if you are confined to a small drawing (fig. 2-13).

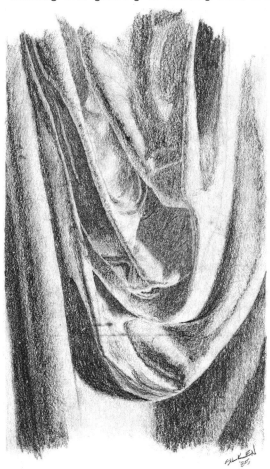

2-12. Life drawing. (Student project by Barbara Silken, University of Oklahoma. Graphite pencil, 12- by 18-inch Strathmore paper.)

2-13. Thumbnail sketching.

SERIAL SKETCHES

Serial sketches are rapidly constructed single-line drawings. They are a bit larger than thumbnail sketches. Four inches by four inches is a good size. For this reason, they can show a little more detail. Draw only enough to capture the character of the space, then stop. Originally they were used to study a sequence of spaces along a given route (fig. 2-14).

ABSTRACTION

To abstract is to reduce to a summary, epitomize, or convey the essential characteristics of a thing. In drawing it is an effort to discard familiar but unnecessary appearances in order to expose and exaggerate the essense of the subject (fig. 2-15).

Pick a subject and draw it. Erase all the trivial details. Exaggerate the important features. Now move the parts around until the usual organization is destroyed.

LETTERING

Along with basic drawing skills, an architect must be able to letter drawings (fig. 2-16). Practice, not prolonged advice here, is needed. A few suggestions may be helpful, however.

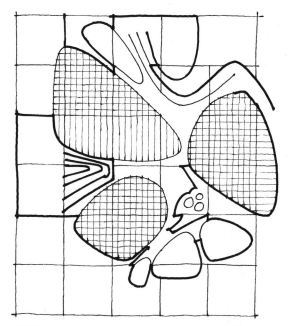

2-15. Abstraction.

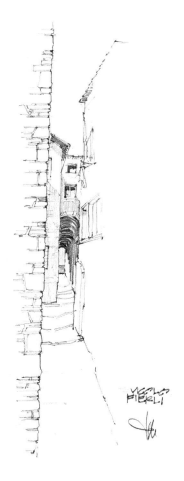

2-14. Serial sketches.

2-16. Typical acceptable alphabets.

Use only one lettering style and one pencil. No one would ever learn to drive if they drove a truck one day and a train the next. Always use your graph paper as a guide. Never try to freehand lettering that is larger than ⅜ inch high. If larger letters are necessary, use transfer type. It is available at your nearest art-supply store. If transfer type seems too expensive or formal, try tracing large letters. For schematic drawings, large freehand letters can be made by first using the broad felt-tip marker and then outlining the letters with a razor-point pen. (fig. 2-17).

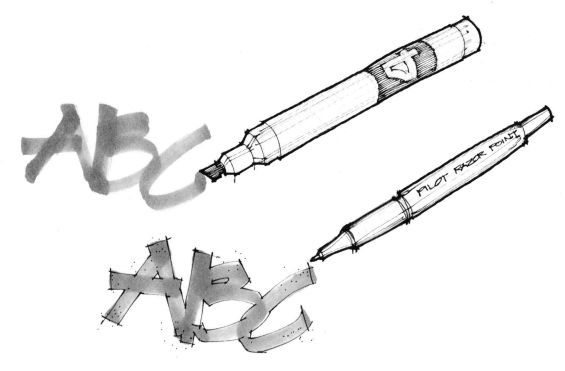

2-17. Lettering with markers.

LANGUAGES AND PHASES 3

The work of most architects follows a predictable pattern. This sequence of design phases progressively matures into the design solution. The client is periodically consulted at various points throughout the process. Depending upon the degree of refinement of the solution at the time, varying types of graphics become appropriate. These are sometimes referred to as graphic languages. Three commonly used languages are schematic, conceptual, and mechanical.

GRAPHIC LANGUAGES
Schematic Language

Some believe in a universe made of things. Others believe in a universe made of forces. Things, like ducks and dogs, have characteristic appearances by which they are recognized. These things invite familiar drawing techniques. Forces are profound in shaping the environment but are much harder to convey. For them, a special graphic language is required. Schematic language is the language of forces or behaviors (fig. 3-1). It is used to show how things act, rather than how they look. With this language a designer can illustrate sun angles, wind direction and velocity, annual temperature variations, job organization, and cash flow (fig. 3-2). This language is also used to study and show how a problem and its solution act.

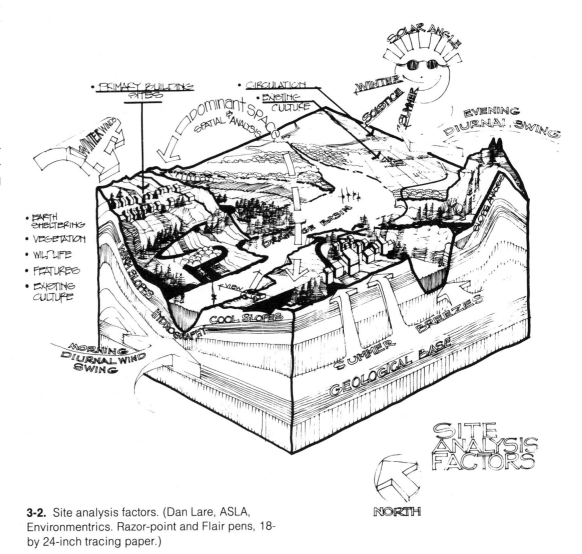

3-1. Schematic language.

3-2. Site analysis factors. (Dan Lare, ASLA, Environmentrics. Razor-point and Flair pens, 18- by 24-inch tracing paper.)

Conceptual Language

Realistic freehand drawings, roughly to scale, are called conceptual drawings (figs. 3-3 and 3-4). They are easily understood by both colleagues and clients. Alternative solutions can be rapidly developed using this language (figs. 3-5 and 3-6). Expressive, realistic drawings of this type require mastery of the skills discussed in chapter 2. Projections (discussed in chapter 5) must also be fully understood in order to employ this language successfully (fig. 3-7). Finally, the artist must understand building construction methods to conceptualize the structure accurately. Too often it is said that a person cannot draw when in fact he actually does not know the materials and details of the thing that is to be built.

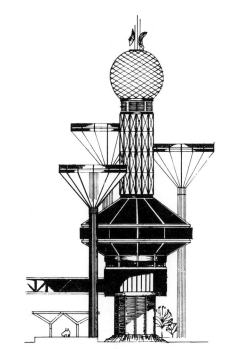

3-3. Conceptual elevation.

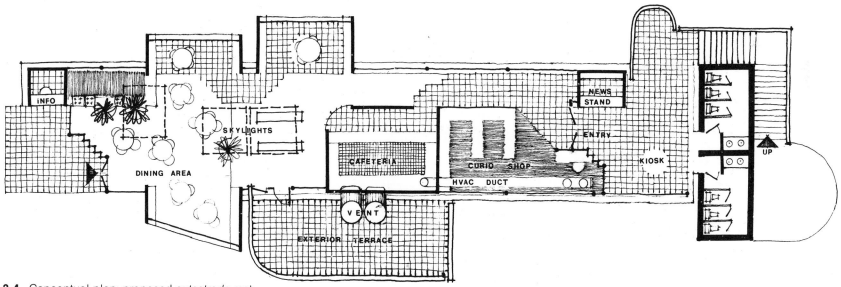

3-4. Conceptual plan: proposed *autostrada* rest area near Siena, Italy. (Graphite pencil on 18- by 24-inch vellum.)

AUTOSTRADA   REST   AREA

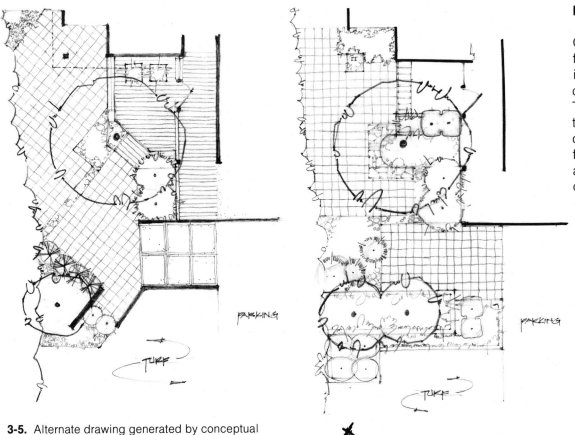

Mechanical Language

Once a solution in the conceptual graphic form has been chosen, the designer moves into the mechanical language. Triangles, compasses, scales, and T squares are used. The main purpose of mechanical drawing is to determine the exact sizes and relationship of components to be certain that the parts will fit together (fig. 3-8). Great care and accuracy are required. Mechanical drawing is time consuming and demands great skill.

3-6. Second alternate drawing generated by conceptual drawing.

3-5. Alternate drawing generated by conceptual drawing.

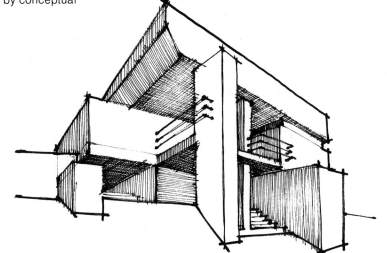

3-7. Conceptual perspective.

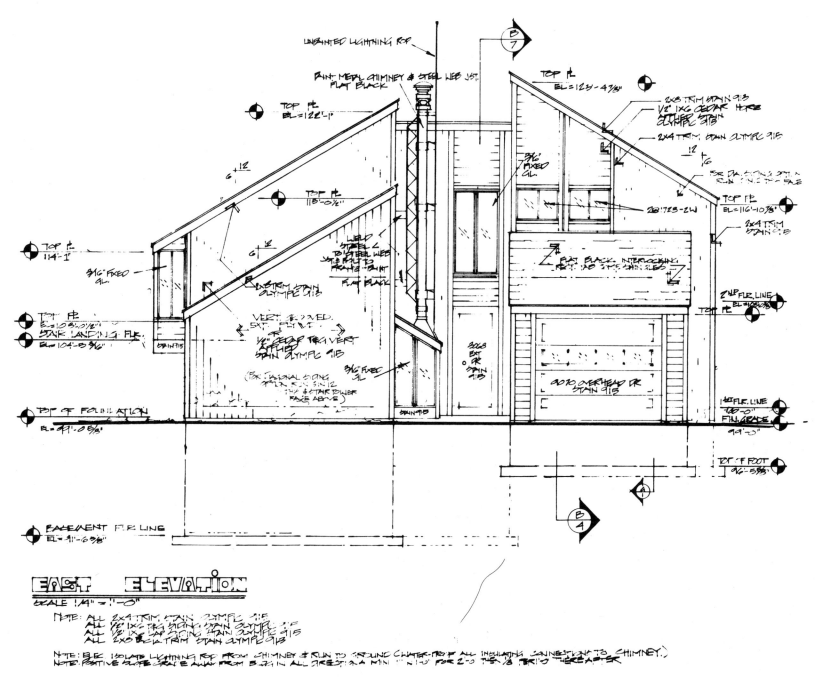

3-8. Mechanical elevation: Haws residence, Springfield, MO.

DESIGN PHASES
Organization Phase

During the organization phase of a project, time, money, and talent are allocated to resolve a specific design problem. Schematic language is appropriate during this phase.

Flow charts. In each design project, specific work activities must be plotted against time. One individual is made responsible for a particular job and the time that job is to be completed is predicted. A flow chart illustrates this (fig. 3-9). Flow charts can also be used to show when and by whom the work was actually executed. Although some job captains prepare flow charts on 8½- by 11-inch paper, it is better to make them wall size and mount them. In this way, a principal, co-worker, or client can evaluate progress on the project at a glance. Everyone has a continuously updated visual work plan to follow (fig. 3-9).

The time strip across the top of the flow chart is a separate piece of paper that is moved forward or backward based on the completion of critical activities in the activity chart below it. Each bubble on the chart represents an activity. The initials of the team member responsible for that part of job are printed in the bubble, along with the target date for completion for that activity. The person actually completing the work signs off in the bubble. (Often this is not the person who was originally assigned the task.) The date of actual completion is also placed in the bubble. For example, if a task was to be done by June 15 by Bob and is not completed until June 20 by Sally, then she initials the bubble when it is completed and writes June 20 in the bubble. The time strip is then adjusted to show that the project is five days behind schedule. The boss is immediately aware of the problem, its source, its magnitude, and who is working the hardest to solve it.

After the project is completed, a work his-

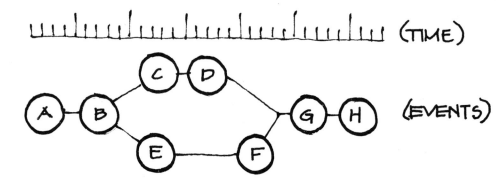

3-9. Work flow chart.

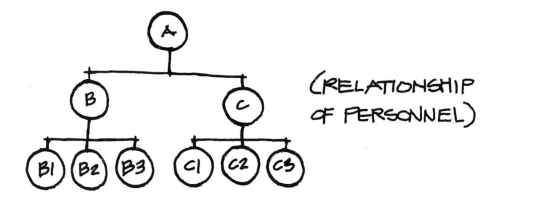

3-10. Organizational chart.

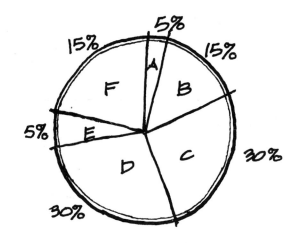

3-11. Pie chart—frequently used to show allocation of time and money.

tory has automatically been recorded. It can be analyzed, and adjustments can be made in future projects. Lazy workers can be identified for personnel action, and good workers can be rewarded.

Personnel charts. A second important schematic visually expresses the relationship of workers on a project (fig. 3-10). It is used to show the organization of power or authority within a design team.

Pie graphs. In order to plan the design process, the budget must be divided between the various design phases. Typically about 60 percent of the design budget will be allocated to the production of working drawings, for example. A pie graph shows how a budget is to be spent (fig. 3-11). At the end of a project, a second pie graph is drawn to show where the money actually was spent. A comparison of the two aids in planning future projects. Firms that consistently compare planned-budget charts with actual-expenditure charts have greater success. They recognize how they spend their time and money and correct any imbalances or overruns.

Research Phase

Once the project has been organized, raw data about the project is collected. Typically a site inventory, including such items as topography, utilities, and climate, will be plotted schematically on a base map (fig. 3-12). The project may also require research into technical areas with which the designer is unfamiliar. Aesthetic issues are also researched at this time. Certainly the client will be consulted concerning functional requirements of the project.

Clients rarely see the mountain of raw data that pours in during this phase; however, the findings must be jointly reviewed by the

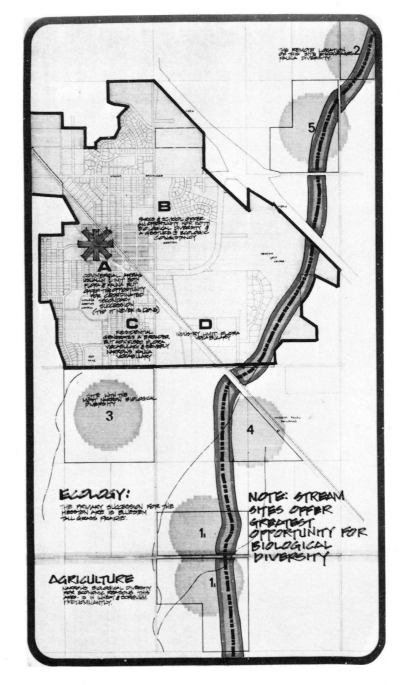

3-12. Overlay on a base map.

whole design team. Schematic graphics are used to visually share research findings.

Where possible, spatially significant data will be placed on a common base map of the site. Other data (such as annual temperature variation) defy such plotting and are reduced to simple charts and diagrams.

A different type of schematic diagram is made by those who research function with the client. They must determine the optimum sizes, shapes, and necessary mechanical support for each required space. Examples of such support include daylight, humidity, and access to hot water. This team also tries to diagram important sequences or relationships among the spaces. These drawings can be schematic (fig. 3-13) or can combine schematic and conceptual drawing (fig. 3-14).

Analysis Phase

The raw data that has been collected must be interpreted. Various means are used to integrate all the isolated data. The designer must also identify the most important issues in the project. Schematic graphics again dominate this phase.

Composite graphic analysis. One of the most powerful means used in this integration of data is the composite graphic analysis (fig. 3-15). All that the designer knows about the problem appears in a single schematic drawing. If a very large sheet is used, much detail may be included. If only a very small sheet is used, trivial issues must be identified and discarded, as only the most critical issues can be shown. Since both sizes have advantages, both should be used.

Because even the large drawings are difficult to see during a presentation, slides are taken of them. The detailed composite graphic analysis will be presented along with the final solution during the design presentation. The composite analysis visually explains the problem, while the design shows the resolution.

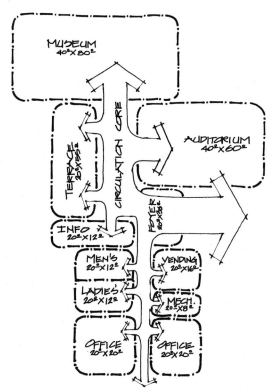

3-13. Functional diagram.

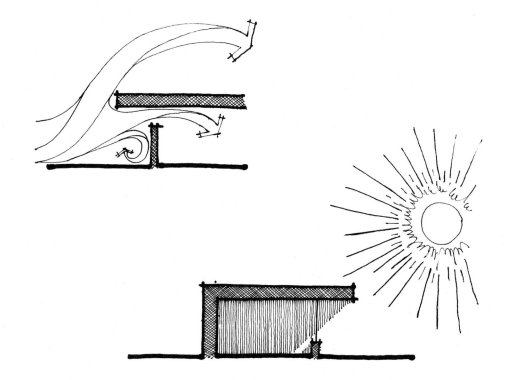

3-14. Some drawings combine schematic and conceptual techniques.

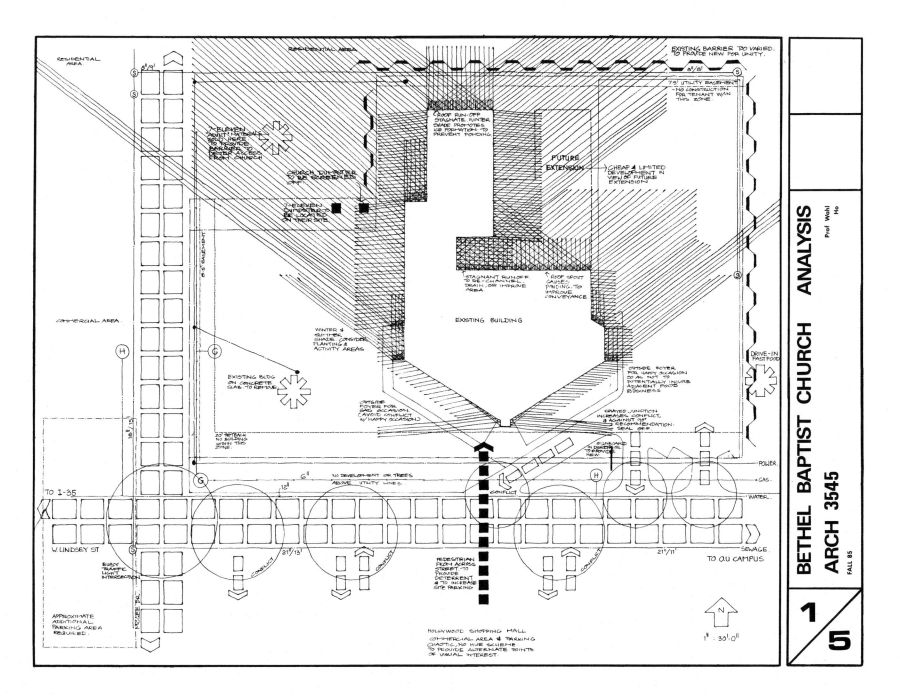

3-15. Composite graphic analysis. (Student project by Ho Yuen Chin, University of Oklahoma. Graphite pencil, 18- by 24-inch vellum.)

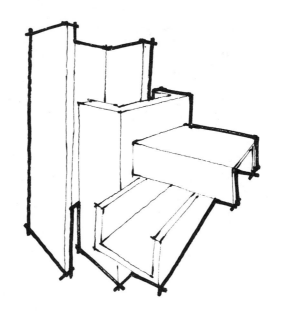

3-16. Abstract idea for a building.

Synthesis Phase

During the synthesis phase, solutions to the problems shown in the composite analysis are explored, first in schematic language and abstract sketches (fig. 3-16) and then in conceptual drawings (fig. 3-17).

A variety of views (projections) are simultaneously developed for each alternative solution. Plans, sections, and elevations are quickly roughed in and then refined (figs. 3-18, 3-19, 3-20, and 3-21). Study models may also be constructed to supplement the drawings. Since clients can easily understand these conceptual drawings and models, they can participate in major decisions. The best solution is chosen.

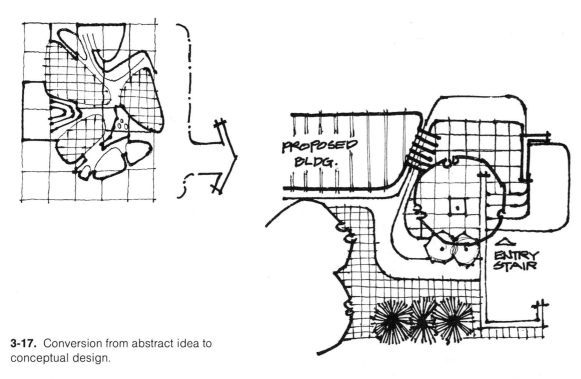

3-17. Conversion from abstract idea to conceptual design.

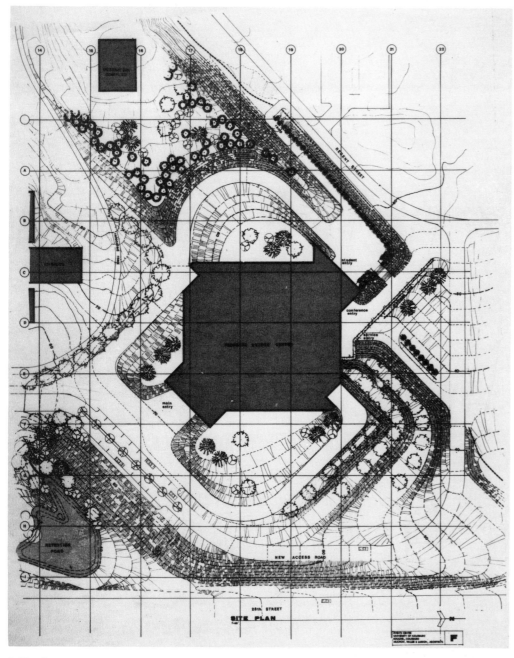

3-18. Conceptual plan: proposed site design for the University of Colorado Events Center. (Prepared by W. C. Muchow Associates, Denver, CO. Technical pencil on 24- by 36-inch Mylar.)

Once the best solution is isolated, conceptual details are developed (figs. 3-22 and 3-23). The whole solution is then converted into a working drawing with mechanical language (fig. 3-24). Mechanical plans, sections, and elevations are completed. As the final presentation date approaches, a mechanical perspective and other presentation drawings will be constructed (figs. 3-25 and 3-26). Often, a final presentation model will also be fabricated.

In a professional office, additional phases are necessary to bring the design to reality, but they will take place after the client says *yes*.

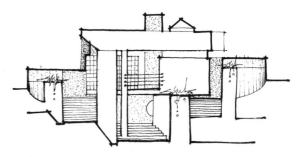

3-19. Conceptual elevation.

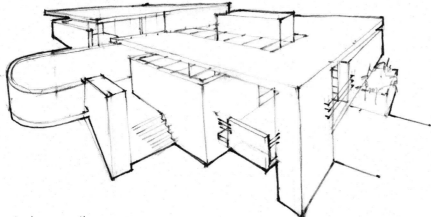

3-20. Conceptual perspective.

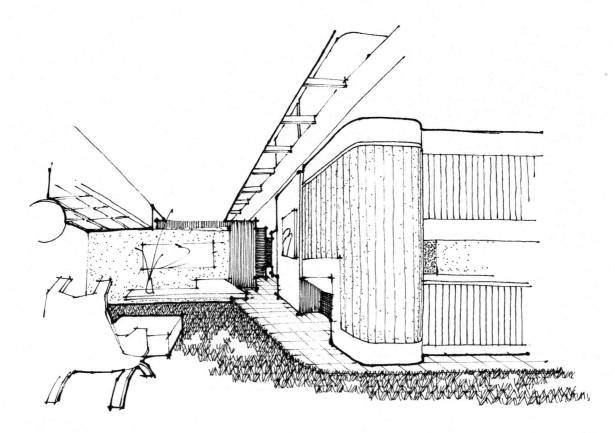

3-21. Conceptual interior.

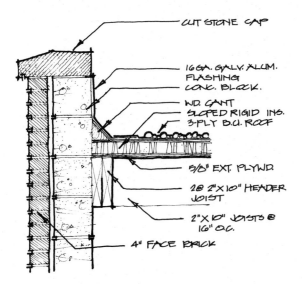

CUT STONE CAP

16 GA. GALV. ALUM. FLASHING

CONC. BLOCK.

WD. CANT

SLOPED RIGID INS.

3-PLY B.U. ROOF

5/8" EXT. PLYWD.

2 @ 2"X10" HEADER JOIST

2"X10" JOISTS @ 16" O.C.

4" FACE BRICK

3-22. Conceptual building detail.

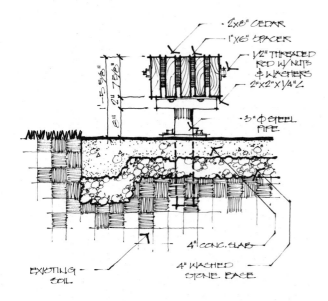

· 2x8" CEDAR

· 1"x6" SPACER

· 1/2" THREADED ROD W/ NUTS & WASHERS

· 2"X2"X1/4" L

· 3" Ø STEEL PIPE

EXISTING SOIL

4" CONC. SLAB

4" WASHED STONE BASE

3-23. Conceptual landscape detail.

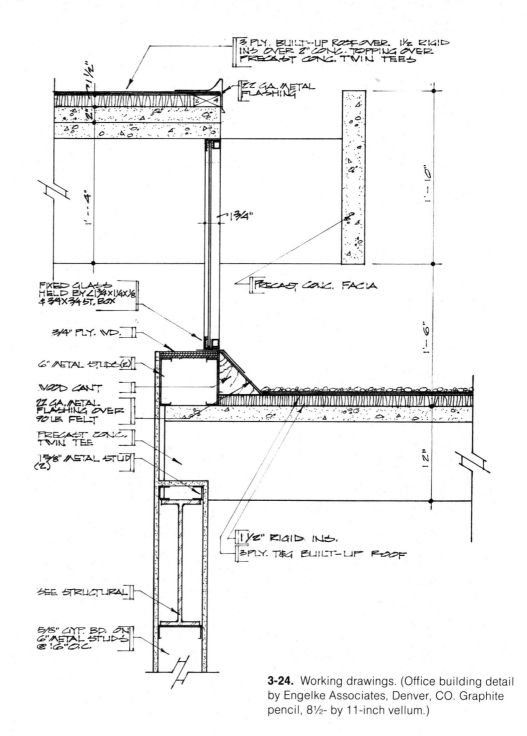

3 PLY. BUILT-UP ROOF OVER. 1½ RIGID INS. OVER 2" CONC. TOPPING OVER PRECAST CONC. TWIN TEES

22 GA. METAL FLASHING

FIXED GLASS HELD BY L1¾X1¼X⅛ & ¾X¾ ST. BOX

3/4" PLY. WD.

6" METAL STUDS (2)

WOOD CANT

22 GA. METAL FLASHING OVER 90 LB. FELT

PRECAST CONC. TWIN TEE

1⅝" METAL STUD (2)

PRECAST CONC. FACIA

1½" RIGID INS.

3 PLY. T&G BUILT-UP ROOF

SEE STRUCTURAL

5/8" GYP. BD. ON 6" METAL STUDS @ 16" O.C.

3-24. Working drawings. (Office building detail by Engelke Associates, Denver, CO. Graphite pencil, 8½- by 11-inch vellum.)

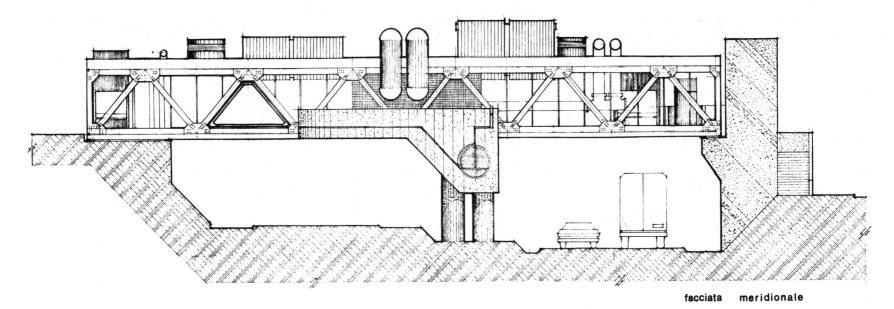

facciata meridionale

3-25. Presentation elevation: proposed *autostrada* rest area near Siena, Italy. (Technical pencil, 12- by 24-inch vellum.)

3-26. Presentation perspective. (Office building by Ed Warner, architect, Denver, CO. Technical pens, 24- by 36-inch vellum.)

COMPOSITION 4

The whole purpose for completing a drawing is to tell the client something. To do this the architect carefully chooses and places visual elements within the boundaries of a picture frame—he composes the drawing.

A choreographer controls a dancer's movements. Similarly the designer hopes to control the movement of the client's eyes and the focus of the client's interest (fig. 4-1). In this way the best aspects of the architect's design are emphasized.

Successful composition achieves the following:

Harmony: Everything in the drawing works together.

Clarity: Your intentions are orderly and clearly stated by the drawing.

Adequacy: The drawing fully conveys the concept behind it. It must be sufficient in both breadth and depth to describe the idea completely.

The following principles of composition are used to achieve these goals:

Emphasis: One element should dominate the drawing. The element chosen conveys the most important thing the designer is trying to tell the client—the idea or concept. There should be a clear hierarchy of importance among the elements in the drawing.

Unity: All the elements should work together toward a single end.

Variety: Variations are purposeful, meaningful differences. All other differences are chaos. Variations show another potential, another viewpoint, another strength (fig. 4-2).

Simplicity/economy: The drawing should convey as much as possible using as little as possible. Alberti said, "Beauty is the condition such that nothing can be added or taken away except to its detriment." Always check to see if the drawing can be improved by subtracting something.

Suitability: All the elements should be relevant, proportional, and appropriate to the idea being conveyed.

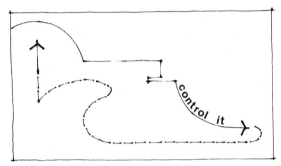

4-1. Control eye movement.

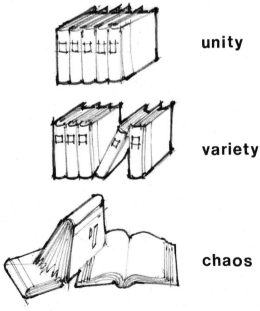

unity

variety

chaos

4-2. Unity versus variety versus chaos.

THEORY OF EXPRESSION

In *A Study in Aesthetics,* Louis Arnaud Reid provides a rational structure for the communication between a designer and a client during a presentation. The following theory of expression is based on his views (fig. 4-3).

The Idea. Designers have lots of ideas. Some of them are expressed easily in words. If that is the case, say them with words. Other ideas and emotions defy words; express these with drawings.

Once the designer is involved in the process of completing a drawing, he too often loses track of the original idea. Worse, some designers never isolate and define the idea in the first place. The idea should always be the driving force behind a drawing; the whole purpose of composition is to focus your client on your concept.

The significance of a design idea has two measures, relevance and innovation. A great drawing of a mediocre idea does not improve the idea by even a gram. The idea must be good before the drawing begins.

Content. The elements of a drawing can be subjective, associative, or objective. Subjective content can be called by name: "It is a duck." Associative content reminds the viewer of something else that can be called by name: "It sure looks like a duck." Objective content appeals to the senses "It is big, red, and loud." The content chosen is based on the idea to be communicated and the needs the idea is intended to communicate.

Subjective content is the most easily understood by a client. Associative is the most dangerous because it is based on the viewer's prior experience, and you cannot know what those experiences were. They may have been unpleasant. Objective content requires careful choice of media. If red is an important part of the idea, it is sensible to choose a medium in which red is possible.

Selecting content requires both quantitative and qualitative decisions. After deciding what will be in the drawing, you must also decide how much, how many, and how big. Try to subtract all the content that you can. Then turn to qualitative questions about color and texture.

Consider your client when choosing content. Dale Carnegie said, "When I fish, I use worms. Personally I like steak, but the fish like worms."

Media. If the idea is strongly three-dimensional, use a model to convey it. If color is important, use watercolor, felt-tip pens, or pastels. If dramatic or reproducible results are significant, use ink. If speed, flexibility, or subtle variations are required, use pencil. Try to master working in as many media as you can; lacking skill in any one can deny it to you as an alternative.

Structure. After originating the idea, choosing the content, and selecting the media, you organize the elements within the space enclosed by the frame. The order may be complex or simple but must never be confused. Use the principles of composition listed earlier to guide you. Elements of order and systems of order are traditional tools that can be used in organizing content. They will be discussed later in this chapter.

The Viewer's Interpretation

Sensing: If the viewer is to interpret your drawing, you must first catch his attention and hold it long enough for the message to be understood.

As soon as you have caught the viewer's attention, he or she will have an initial sensory reaction. This occurs before any meaning is interpreted. The response can be pleasant or unpleasant.

Meaning. If the viewer's senses have not been offended, he will try to make sense out of the object. The interpretation will be based on the current context, the viewer's past experience, and the content and organization of the drawing. The interpretation may be perfect or imperfect, depending on both the viewer and the viewing circumstances. If the viewer cannot interpret the drawing, he will either arbitrarily assign meaning to it or he will stop looking at it. Either way, the communication—and the designer—will have failed.

Importance. The viewer will decide if your drawing is important based on the meaning he interprets. If it is trivial, it will be dismissed, the process will end, and once again the designer will have failed.

Skill in workmanship and labor expended lend significance to the drawing and demand that it be considered seriously.

Appetite. If the viewer has come this far, the drawing, with all its content, will be subjected to taste. Taste, or individual appetite, is a child of past experiences. Some were pleasant, some were not.

Expression (done by designer)				Interpretation (done by viewer)				
Idea	Content	Media	Structure	Sensing	Meaning	Importance	Taste	Beauty
Relevant or irrelevant	Subjective	2-dimensional: Watercolor	Principles of composition	Attract attention or fail to attract attention	Understand or misunderstand	Profound or trivial	Satisfy appetites or not satisfy appetites	Like it or not like it
	Associative	Pencil						
Innovative or banal	Objective	Ink Etc.	Elements of order					
		3-dimensional: Model Samples Etc.	Systems of order	Directly please the senses or directly offend the senses				
		4-dimensional: Film Videotape Etc.						

4-3. Process of expression.

If the design must be approved by more than one person, it will also be subject to fashion—that is, group taste. It is easier to satisfy one person's taste than many people's.

Beauty. Beauty is an emotional response based on judgment. Obviously, beauty is difficult to achieve. Do you really need it? The answer is yes, for many reasons, the primary one being that it is a powerful tool in obtaining approval from your client.

ELEMENTS OF CONTENT

Developing an adequate literacy in visual expression—understanding the components that make up a design—is a critical step in gaining skill in presentation. Donis Dondis's *A Primer of Visual Literacy* can be very helpful in this study. Some of the elements of content a designer may choose in creating a drawing are defined below.

Space. Space provides the opportunity for something to happen. Some designers think of it only as the white part of the paper that is not filled with objects. If this were true, space in a composition would be no more important than the dough that is left over after a baker cuts out his cookies. This viewpoint wrongly accepts the objects as important, treating the remaining space as useless. Architects often refer to the objects as "masses" and the spaces as "voids." The most important thing to remember about spaces or voids is that the design of spaces is as important as the design of the objects that fill space. Neither has meaning without the other. Just as the mass of the objects can be changed in size and shape, so can the voids.

Point. A point is a position in space. A *focal point* is the location of greatest emphasis, interest, and attention in a drawing. A counterpoint is a second area of strong interest introduced into a drawing to achieve balance and to provide a sense of movement (fig. 4-4).

Do not confuse any of the above with focus of the viewer's eyes. The focus of the viewer's eyes changes constantly as they shift about from instant to instant to take in all of the drawings. Control of this movement guides composition.

Line. A line is the path of a moving point (fig. 4-5). It is your most powerful tool in focusing the viewer's eyes with considerable predictability.

Lines are like vectors: they have starting points (origins), directions, force, and velocity. They give the viewer a "ride" just as if he were watching a pilot perform acrobatics at an air show. Some rides are dime rides, like riding the bus. Other rides are worth more, like rides at an amusement park. The type of "ride" you choose depends on the idea you are pursuing. Roller coaster lines seem wrong in a rendering for a mortuary.

POINT — A POSITION

FOCAL POINT — LOCATION OF GREATEST EMPHASIS

COUNTERPOINT — LOCATION OF SIGNIFICANT SECONDARY EMPHASIS

4-4. Point, focal point, and counterpoint.

LINE — PATH OF A MOVING POINT

STRAIGHT LINE — PATH OF A MOVING POINT THAT DOESN'T CHANGE DIRECTION

IMPLIED LINE — MAKES FOCUS OF EYES FOLLOW A PREDICTABLE ROUTE

4-5. Line, straight line, and implied line.

A straight line is the path of a moving point that does not change direction.

An implied line is not continuous; sometimes it is not even visible. It focuses the viewer's eyes on a predictable path without being continuous. Think of it as a dotted line.

Shape. A shape is a two-dimensional object bounded by a closed line (fig. 4-6).

An *outline* is that enclosing line without the enclosed substance. A *silhouette* is the two-dimensional substance of a shape, without the outline. A *geometric shape* is a specifically defined form—for example, a square, rectangle, triangle, or parallelogram—used in mathematics as well as art.

When shapes overlap in space, they generate *critical edges*. If these edges are not emphasized or clarified, the two planes appear to "merge," causing the viewer considerable confusion.

Plane. A plane is usually a flat surface, although it can bend or warp on occasion (fig. 4-7).

Form. A form is the three-dimensional equivalent of shape (fig. 4-8). When seen at a distance, a form appears to be two-dimensional. Consequently forms share many characteristics with shapes, specifically outline, silhouette, and critical edge.

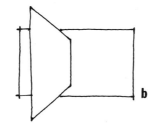

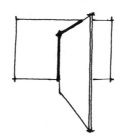

4-7. *a.* Plane. *b.* Overlapping planes generate critical edges.

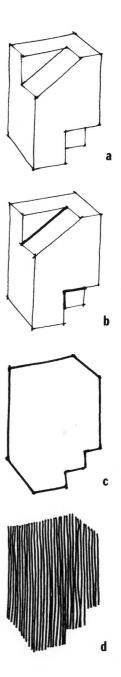

4-8. *a.* Form. *b.* Critical edges on a form. *c.* Outline of a form. *d.* Silhouette of a form.

SHAPE — TWO-DIMENSIONAL OBJECT ENCLOSED BY A CLOSED LINE

OUTLINE — ENCLOSES A SHAPE

SILHOUETTE — TWO-DIMENSIONAL SUBSTANCE OF A SHAPE

GEOMETRIC SHAPE — SPECIAL, LIMITED FAMILY OF SHAPES ROOTED IN MATHEMATICS

4-6. Shape, outline, silhouette, and geometric shape.

Mass is often used to refer to gross volumes without details and surface treatments. It implies more than *volume* because it implies weight.

Texture. Texture is a visual indication of tactile roughness. *Grain* describes the individual elements that constitute a surface, whether it is a brick or a piece of sand. Texture actually describes the variation among the grains combined on a given surface. Both grain and texture are measured relatively with terms such as coarse, medium, and fine. Note that coarse grains combined with other coarse grains make *fine* texture because they are all the same size. To make coarse texture you must combine coarse with fine grains (fig. 4-9).

Pattern results if the grains are organized in some predictable and orderly way. In a pattern equal objects are spaced equally on a surface (such as wallpaper). Patterns are extendable: if you need to buy two more feet of a certain wallpaper, you could predict its exact appearance. The opposite is also true. If a piece was cut from your wallpaper, a stranger would know exactly what was missing.

Light. The effects of light on an object can be classified into light, shade, and shadow. The side of an object on which direct light falls is said to be lighted. The opposite side is said to be in shade. Because light cannot pass through the object, a shadow may be cast on surfaces adjacent to the object. Light is a powerful visual tool used to reveal form (fig. 4-10).

Color. Color is generally classified by hue, value, and chroma. In imprecise layman's terms, a *hue* is the name by which we identify a color in its pure unmixed state (such as red or blue). In practice many painters call red, yellow, and blue *primary hues* because *secondary hues* (orange, purple, and green) and

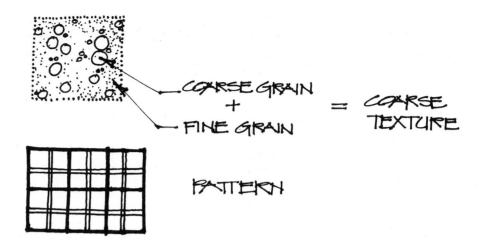

4-9. *top:* Grain and texture. *bottom:* Pattern.

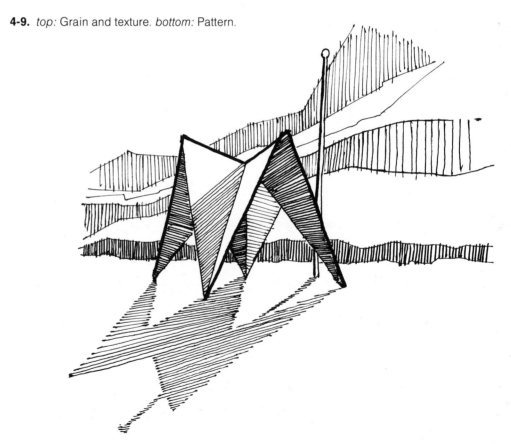

4-10. Light reveals form.

tertiary hues (such as red-orange and blue-green) can all be mixed from these three primary hues. In order to experiment with hues, buy a color wheel at an art-supply store. It will cost less than five dollars and will be quite helpful in choosing an appropriate hue scheme. Fortunately a limited number of hue schemes are commonly used (figs. 4-11 and 4-12).

Value describes the lightness and darkness of a color (figs. 4-11 and 4-12). A black-and-white photo will show you the values of a scene without the interference of hue and chroma. A great many renderings fail to include this aspect of color adequately. If you squint hard or look at your drawing, you can reduce the *intensity* of the hues enough to be more aware of the size and placement of values. Dark values give the appearance of weight and are important for balance and emphasis in a drawing.

Chroma describes the intensity or purity of color. High chroma adds energy to a drawing, like shoving the accelerator to the floor when you are driving—better be sure you can handle it. If you add white paint to red paint, it will not only lighten in value, but it also becomes less intense. This is a *tint*. If you added black paint to the red paint, it darkens in value and again becomes less intense. This is a *tone*. Together, tints and tones are called *shades*.

Colors are also said to have *temperature*. Reds, yellows, and oranges are considered warm colors; blue and green are considered cool.

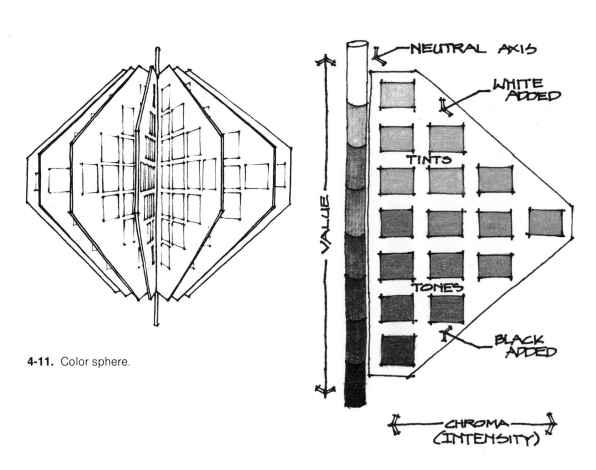

4-11. Color sphere.

4-12. Example from the color sphere.

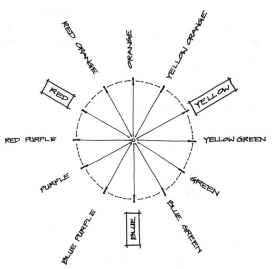

4-13. The color wheel is the color sphere seen from above. Note the neutral axis at the center.

ELEMENTS OF ORDER

Elements of order are used to aid in structuring or organizing the content in a drawing.

Balance. Balance is equal apparent weight and visual interest on both sides of a given axis, usually at the middle of the drawing (fig. 4-14).

Symmetry or *formal balance* requires mirrored images on both sides of an axis. *Asymmetry* or *informal balance* requires equal but different treatment on both sides of an axis. Symmetry has greater power, while asymmetry will sustain a viewer's interest for a longer period.

Proportion. Proportion involves meaningful relationships of parts to the whole, the whole to its parts, and the parts to each other (fig. 4-15). It differs from scale in that the comparisons are self-contained.

Scale. Scale involves a comparison to any preconceived measure. Human scale compares an object to the human body. Contextual scale compares the object to the things around it (fig. 4-16).

Dominance. A clear hierarchy of size and importance in a drawing makes your meaning more apparent. What is most important? What is the next most important? You should be able to list the elements in order of importance—or dominance—before you start drawing (fig. 4-17).

Similarity. Humans automatically relate like objects in their mind. Similar shapes and colors are particularly assertive (fig. 4-18).

Proximity. Humans also relate objects that are placed close together. They want to believe that they are not accidentally in this condition (fig. 4-19).

Sequence. Objects in space can be placed to form a predictable succession. Such a succession of objects is extendable at either end. Dissimilar objects can be related using this technique. If properly done, a viewer will know if something is missing from the sequence (fig. 4-20).

Repetition. Repetition is anything . . . again: two like objects, a mirror image, the same note played twice. Often it is done to "burn" something into the viewer's consciousness (fig. 4-21).

4-17. Dominance.

4-18. Similarity.

4-19. Proximity.

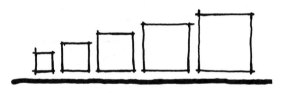

4-20. Sequence.

4-21. Repetition.

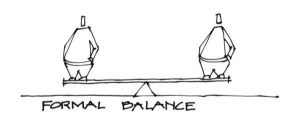

4-14. Balance.

4-15. Bad proportion.

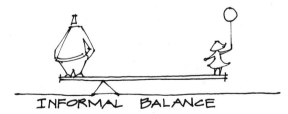

4-16. Scale.

SYSTEMS OF ORDER

Over the years some traditional arrangements of elements in drawings have evolved. Viewers are consequently conditioned to look for them and recognize them easily. Here are a few of the most common.

Rhythm. Rhythm is a special type of repetition. In a drawing it is usually the result of the linear grouping of similar elements at predictable intervals on the page. Rhythm is similar to pattern in space. (In fact, the space between figures on wallpaper is also called an interval.) Usually if something happens only twice, it is not recognized as rhythm. When a third repetition is perceived, it's no accident, and predictability begins. Like patterns, rhythms are also extendable (fig. 4-22).

Trends. Predictability that is not based on repetition results in a trend. Two common examples are *crescendo* and *diminuendo,* both of which are music terms. A crescendo is a progressively intensified experience (as in music getting louder). Diminuendo is the opposite of crescendo—a decrease in intensity.

4-22. Rhythm.

In a perspective drawing, it happens automatically as objects approach a vanishing point in the distance.

Theme. The theme is the underlying idea, slogan, topic, or melody of a piece. Usually it invites variations (fig. 4-23).

Geometric Organization. Geometric organization involves the arrangement of elements in a path that resembles a common shape (fig. 4-24). Typical examples include *circular, triangular,* and *axial* organization.

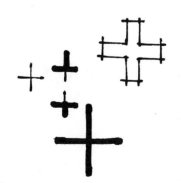

4-23. Theme.

Circular and triangular organization focus viewers' eyes along a simple, self-renewing, preplanned path. (Self-renewing means the path is endless and continuous—the viewer will make the circuit more than once. In an axial organization, elements are arranged along a line.)

Undulation. Undulation involves the organization of elements along a sensuous but often unrenewed preplanned path in a painting.

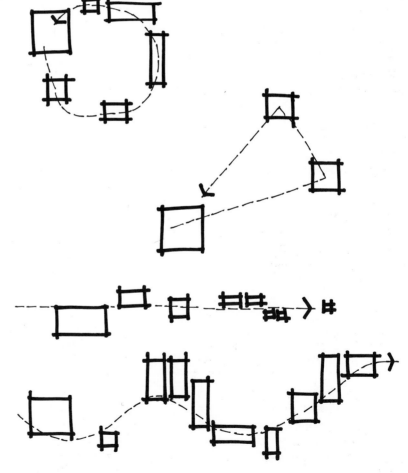

4-24. Common geometric arrangements.

STEP-BY-STEP COMPOSITION

Begin by *making a plan.* First, clarify the underlying idea or purpose for doing the drawing. Try the basic interrogatives: answer who, what, why, when, where, and how much. If this does not work, try "why chaining." Ask "Why is this drawing necessary?" and answer. Then ask, "But why is that?" and answer. Again ask, "But why is that?" If you are still having problems, find a friend and explain in exacting detail what you are trying to accomplish and why that is so critical. Once you are able to explain your idea clearly in about 2,000 words, get down to the minimum. Explain your purpose in a short sentence. A little work now saves a lot of work—and mistakes—later. A single clear concept will automatically encourage unity and emphasis in the final drawing since it pursues only one idea.

Next, *choose your content.* Decide on building view, character of the site, the activities of the people, and the types of vehicles that are appropriate. Consider both your theme and your audience when choosing content. Also decide how you will treat objective content—color, texture, and the like—which is always part of a drawing. Be specific in preliminary planning for these. Later studies may shift your thinking, but you should start with a plan. For example, know whether you are going to do a dramatic high-value scheme with no color or a subtle monochromatic rendering with little value and textural variation.

Now *make your projection.* Choose the type of projection that you need. For example, is a two-point mechanical perspective required, or will a quick asymmetrical dimetric be sufficient? Quickly cast the general masses of your design to see if you have chosen the right view (fig. 4-25). If you are satisfied, draw

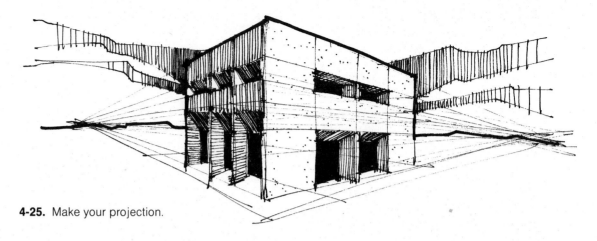

4-25. Make your projection.

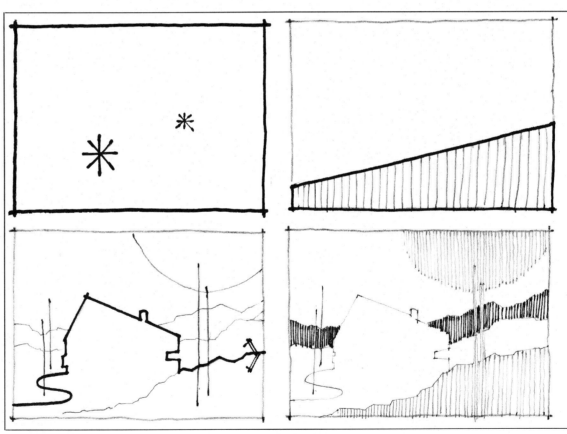

4-26. Study the composition with overlays.

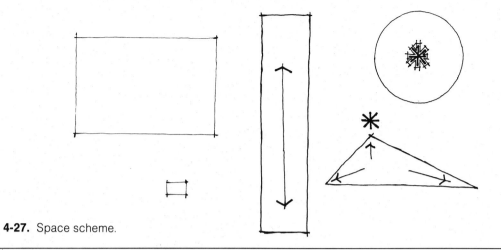

4-27. Space scheme.

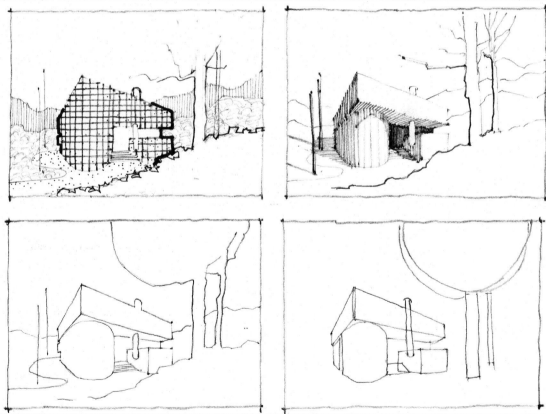

4-26, *continued.*

in the details too. If you find that you have chosen the wrong projection, quickly make a study of a different view or projection.

As previously discussed, *select your media* (ink, pencil, or whatever you prefer). Do not forget to choose the type of paper you will use. With transparent papers you can trace entourage and your projection. You cannot do this with presentation boards; they require more time, skill, and care as well. If your media choice includes running some prints, remember to allow sufficient time for this task.

Before you begin the final drawing, *prepare studies with schematic overlays*. Develop quick 8½- by 11-inch overlays, one for each of the elements of content discussed earlier in this chapter (fig. 4-26). The first of the overlay studies should depict space scheme (fig. 4-27). Does your drawing space have assertive corners to compete with your drawing? Does it already have directional movement that can be exploited? Does the space restrict the shape and size of content? It is hard to draw an overweight elephant on a narrow vertical piece of paper. Also consider the hue, texture, and value of the paper before you begin. Does your paper already have a strongly implied focal point?

Next study the point scheme. Locate your intended focal point (fig. 4-28); divide your paper into either thirds or fifths both vertically and horizontally. Usually the focal point is placed at one of the intersections of these dividing lines. The center of the sheet is usually the worst choice. Locate a counterpoint if you need one. Check the balance. The line scheme is the most critical in exciting and controlling movement (fig. 4-29). Remember, vertical lines are assertive and attract attention. Horizontal lines are used for continuity, to tie things together. Diagonal lines generate drama—use them sparingly, and check

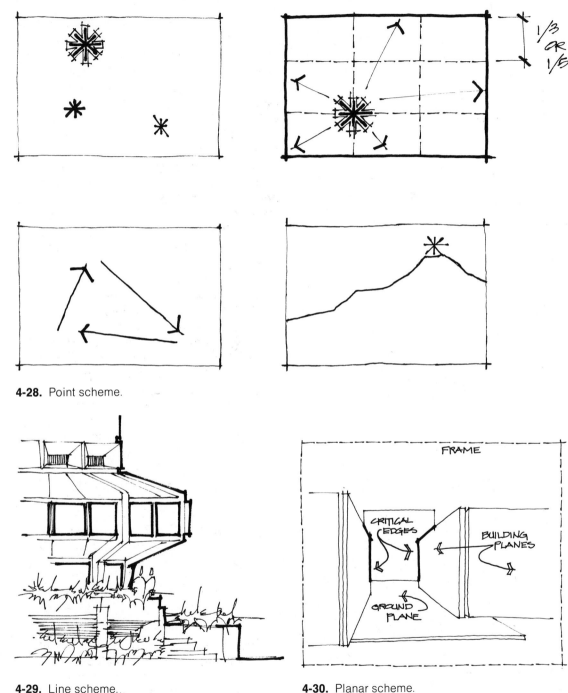

4-28. Point scheme.

4-29. Line scheme.

4-30. Planar scheme.

your balance again if they are introduced. Shadows often cast diagonal lines that are forgotten. In the hierarchy of lines, the sky line is often most important. The outside edge of a rendering can also become significant if a strong dark medium is used.

Study the planar scheme (fig. 4-30). It establishes, encloses, molds, and modulates space in the imaginary world of your drawing. This is another opportunity to move the viewer. Coordinate it closely with the line scheme movements. Mark all critical edges to avoid confusing the viewer. Coordination of planar schemes with the texture scheme will allow you to differentiate overlapping surfaces.

The shape scheme study should not only show the obvious shapes of buildings, but should also examine less obvious shapes such as clouds, trees, and other entourage you intend to include (fig. 4-31). Determine a hierarchy of sizes in these shapes. Also decide if rectangles, circles, or triangles will dominate the rendering. If your drawing is made predominantly of rectangles and you include one lone circle, the circle will become a focal point.

The analysis of the texture scheme will allow you to study grain, texture, and pattern simultaneously (fig. 4-32). Do not use abrupt contrasts of texture (coarse and fine). Instead, make transitions from one texture to another. You will have to respect the actual material that you are representing while considering the light and value schemes as well. Coarse textures are assertive and will become focal points. They also add energy to a drawing. A small drawing cannot support much of this strong texture.

Study the effects of light (fig. 4-33). Light will help reveal the sculptural forms in your drawing. Since light involves shade and shadow, it will have a strong impact on the

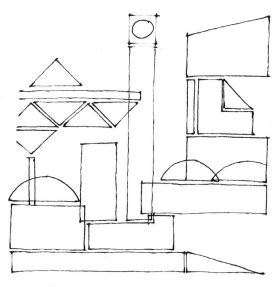

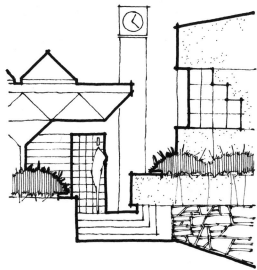

4-31. Shape scheme.

value scheme you will soon develop. It is usually best to combine the effects of light with the textural necessities dictated by the materials in your drawing (fig. 4-34). Show more texture in shaded areas. This simultaneously conveys the material and its lighting. Later, when color washes are placed over this surface, this increased texture will automatically modify the intensity and value of the color used.

The hue scheme is often the most difficult to plan. Go to your nearest art-supply store and buy a cheap color wheel. It is the best buy you will ever make. Read the instructions and follow them. They will help you choose one of the following hue schemes (fig. 4-35):

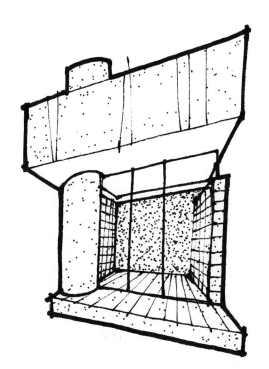

4-32. Texture scheme.

4-33. Light scheme.

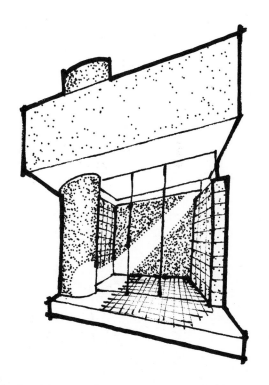

4-34. Combine the effects of light and texture.

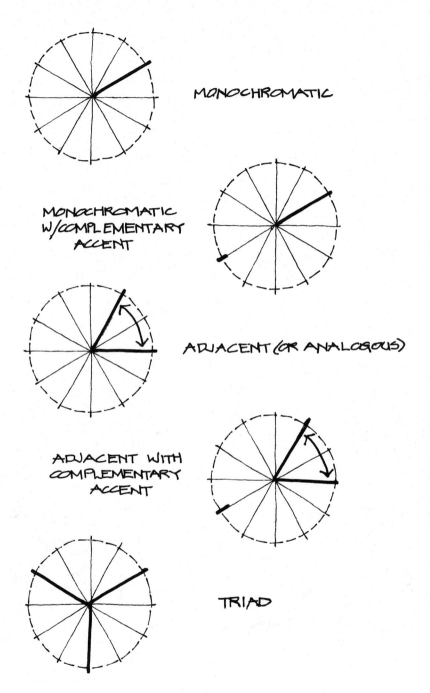

MONOCHROMATIC

MONOCHROMATIC
W/COMPLEMENTARY
ACCENT

ADJACENT (OR ANALOGOUS)

ADJACENT WITH
COMPLEMENTARY
ACCENT

TRIAD

4-35. Alternate hue schemes.

Monochromatic: Shades of one color only. Often, even the paper is a mild tint of the color selected. Brown or warm gray monochromatic schemes can get pretty dull; try adding a dash of orange or yellow to enliven them a bit.

Monochromatic with a complementary accent: Shades of one color with just a dash of the color directly opposite on the color wheel. Usually, most of the drawing is kept drab. The accent, small and intense, should be located at the drawing's focal point.

Adjacent: Pick two colors that are directly adjacent on the color wheel, blue and green for example. Render only in shades of these colors. Be sure one of the colors dominates the other.

Adjacent with a complementary accent: Some call this a near split. It is begun like the adjacent scheme just described; however, a dash of the hue directly opposite on the color wheel is then added. Drab shades of the adjacent hues are used for most of the drawing; the complementary accent is intense and is placed near the drawing's focal point.

Triad: Three hues equally spaced around the color wheel (such as red, yellow, and blue). Maintaining color hierarchy is critical in triad schemes. The more intense you allow the colors to become, the more you court disaster. Since black, white, and gray are neutral colors that can be used without interfering with these schemes, many will do a render that is a study in grays, and then introduce a triad in small but intense accents to enliven the drawing.

The alternative hue schemes listed above begin with the easiest to use and become progressively difficult and dangerous to handle as you approach the triad. When in doubt, start with a good line drawing. Choose the most simple hue scheme that your design will allow. Treat the line drawing like a children's coloring book. Lightly and evenly apply the chosen hues to the line drawing. Do not be afraid to leave lots of white space in the drawing. Do not color anything that is not absolutely necessary. Can you get away with a monochromatic? If not, try a monochromatic with a complementary accent. Be cowardly with color in the beginning. If it works, quit (see fig. C-9 in the color insert).

Study the value scheme next (fig. 4-36). You can do this with tones built up in pencil or with felt-tip markers in shades of gray. The focal point will be where the whitest white is adjacent to the darkest gray. Since value adds weight to a drawing, restudy the balance carefully at this time. You should plan to include the brightest white, darkest dark, and medium tones in every rendering. Try using the white of the paper, a warm gray #4 marker, and a black felt-tip marker to make this study. Your drawing will have a foreground, middle ground, and background. You also are using three values for your study. Try all the possible variations until the best is found. There are only nine ways to shuffle the values around between the various grounds, so this is an easy task.

The chroma or intensity scheme is best understood by looking at an example (see fig. C-10 in the color insert). The purpose of this schematic is to isolate the study of chroma from the complexities of hue. It is done with one intense felt-tip pen (red is good), a white Prismacolor pencil, and a warm gray Prisma pencil. This converts the drawing into a monochromatic drawing in shades of red. For ex-

ample, if an object in the drawing is to be intense blue, color it intense *red.* If another object is to be intense green, color it intense *red.* A dull tint of any hue becomes a dull tint in *red.* A very light tint of any color becomes a light tint of *red* in this study. When you are finished with drawing, you will be able to identify the focal point in the intensity scheme. Confirm that it coincides with the focal point in the value scheme.

Now *refine the entourage* in your drawing. Add the trees, cars, people, and furniture exactly as you intend to include them in the drawing. Chapter 6 should help you accomplish this refinement.

Finally *complete the rendering in its final media.* Whether you use pencil, pastels, ink, or watercolor, you will probably need to practice a bit. Chapter 7 will provide additional guidance for this final step.

4-36. Value scheme.

PROJECTIONS 5

Presentations begin with a choice of a projection. The choice of view is based on which features in the rendering the designer wishes to emphasize or explain. The projection chosen is that which shows these features to their best advantage. Projections fall into two main categories, paraline and perspective. The lines in a perspective projection converge on a point (or points). The lines in a paraline projection do not.

PARALINE PROJECTIONS

Paraline projections consist primarily of *orthographic* drawings, *axonometric* drawings, and *oblique* drawings. These, in turn, are further classified. Orthographic drawings may be *plans, sections,* or *elevations* (fig. 5-1). Axonometric drawings are *isometric, dimetric* (either symmetrically or asymmetrically), or *trimetric* (fig. 5-2). Oblique drawings are categorized as *cavalier, general, cabinet,* and *plan* (fig. 5-3).

The most useful of these are the orthographic views and the isometric and asymmetrical dimetric views. Orthographics (plans, sections, and elevations) are used for working drawings which guide the contractor in actual fabrication. Isometrics are used to show complex details and for aerial views of complex urban sites. Asymmetrical dimetrics are quick, easy substitutes for perspectives. Several types are possible, but the one illustrated in figure 5-2 is the easiest to draw. You will need an adjustable triangle to make best use of it, however. The advantage of this projection is that dimensions may be directly scaled in the drawing. If a side is to be eight feet long, it will either be scaled directly at that length or divided by two, as indicated.

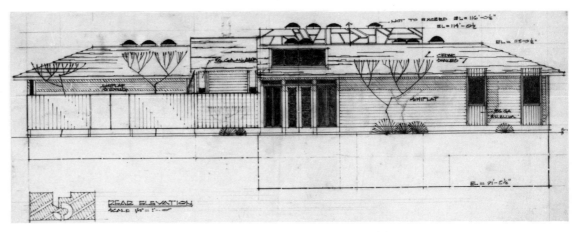

5-1. Orthographic drawing, elevation: Burt Welz residence, Littleton, CO.

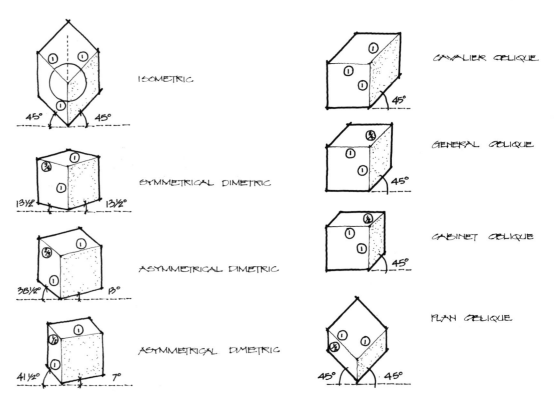

5-2. Axonometric drawings.

5-3. Oblique drawings.

PERSPECTIVES

All perspectives are converging line projections (fig. 5-4). Perspectives are classified as one, two, or three point, based on the number of points upon which lines converge (fig. 5-5). Since the two-point perspective is the type most often used, it will be the one discussed in this chapter.

Perspectives are also grouped into those that are constructed by freehand and those that are constructed mechanically. Reading various sources on the subject can therefore be quite confusing. Many methods of perspective drawing have been proposed, and while each has its strength, many are not very useful. For this reason, only one freehand and one mechanical method will be discussed at length in this book.

Freehand perspectives are design tools. Since they can be rapidly and easily drawn and are reasonably accurate, they can aid in developing a design solution. Mechanical perspectives require completed plan and elevation drawings. This means that the design must already be complete. Therefore, they are used only as presentation tools.

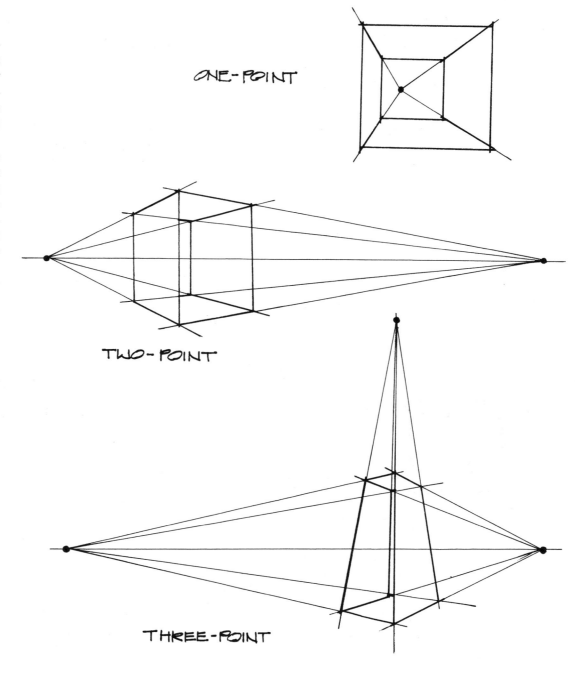

ONE-POINT

TWO-POINT

THREE-POINT

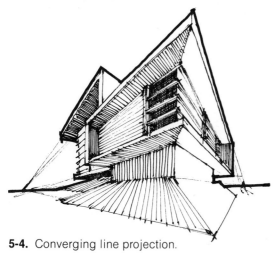

5-4. Converging line projection.

5-5. One-, two-, and three-point perspectives.

Freehand Perspectives

Use your clipboard and graph paper to aid you in learning to draw freehand perspectives. William Kirby Lockard has given considerable effort to explaining and popularizing this skill; read his excellent book *Design Drawing Experiences* for more detailed guidance.

All systematic freehand methods are based on two assumptions: first, that people can draw a three-dimensional cube in space; and second, that a size (usually 10 by 10 by 10 feet) can be assigned to such a cube.

This single cube is then multiplied in all directions to form a three-dimensional grid in space (fig. 5-6). Designed objects can be drawn within the grid. Since the grid is "scaled" in ten-foot increments, plans and elevations can then be drawn from this object-filled grid.

More than one method can be used to achieve the three-dimensional expansion of the original cube. The more recent edition of Lockard's book returns to the "method of diagonals," which is periodically rediscovered. Very little remains to be added to Lockard's capable work; however, students have found the sequential drawings in figure 5-7 helpful in learning this important skill. Once this freehand method is mastered, the position of the original cube can be modified to be seen from above, below, from the left, or from the right. Although best used as a design tool, this method can also be used to construct simple, small, relatively crude presentation drawings.

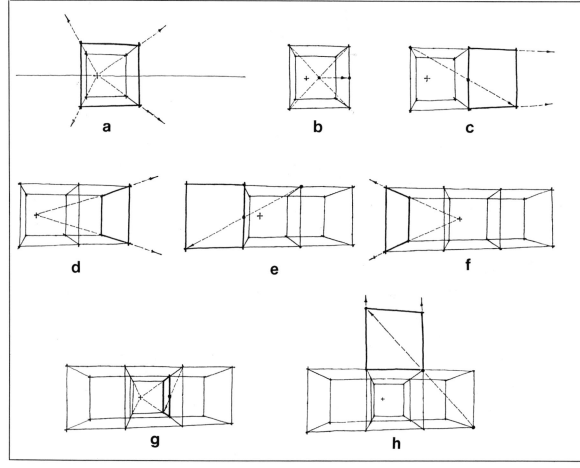

5-6. Freehand perspective grid.

5-7. Cube-expansion sequence.

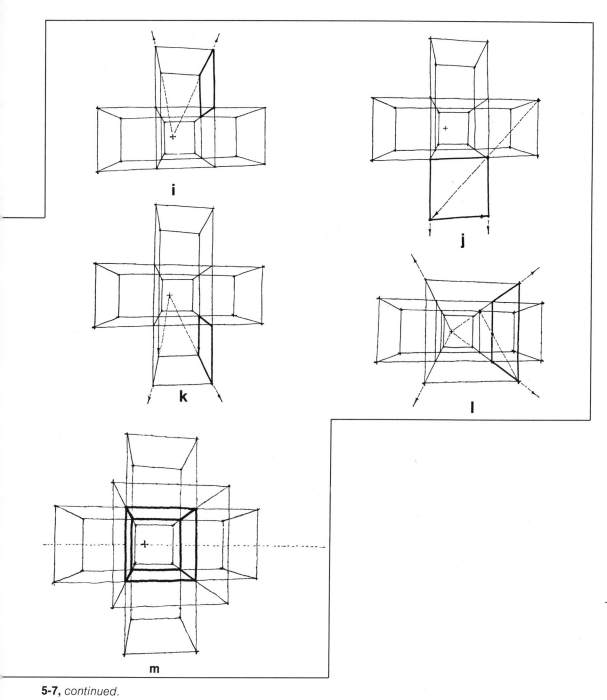

i

j

k

l

m

5-7, continued.

Only six skills (fig. 5-8) are necessary to master this technique:

1. Drawing a straight line.
2. Connecting corners to the vanishing point.
3. Drawing diagonals to find the vertical and horizontal center of a cube.
4. Drawing a second type of diagonal through the midpoint of any side of a cube. We will use these to expand the original cube in that direction.
5. Drawing lines that converge on an imaginary point off the edge of your paper. This allows the grid to have a second vanishing point, without becoming too exaggerated. If you cannot do this, do not be too worried —just use your graph paper and draw the lines parallel. Although limited, this is better than abandoning this useful projection.
6. Visually judging the depth of any side of a cube so that the side is square in perspective. That is to say, it is ten feet high and ten feet wide, although foreshortening will occur in any perspective.

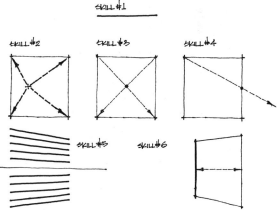

5-8. The six basic skills needed for expanding a cube.

Mechanical Perspectives

On occasion, one-point perspectives are used for interior design and three-point perspectives are used for very tall buildings. However, the two-point perspective is by far the most widely used (fig. 5-9).

Methods for mechanically drawing perspectives abound. Some resemble the freehand method just described, in that they call for drawing a lot of grids or graphs prior to locating the actual design. The method presented in the following paragraphs requires you to draw only those few lines that you really need. (Note: Do not mix books and methods in perspective—this leads to disaster.)

While the results of this method are stunning, the construction process appears to be very difficult. Very few books actually proceed step by step through the process. Skim through the following process briefly, and do not be intimidated or bored. Just skim it. Next time you have a real need for a perspective, get this chapter out and proceed step by step following the instructions. Before you begin, look at the results of the completed process. It is often easier to follow a route, if you already know where it leads (fig. 5-10).

Step 1: Complete the plan and elevation drawings in the scale that will fit on your board (fig. 5-11). Be certain they are in the same scale.

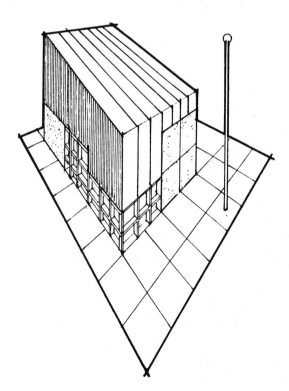

5-9. Two-point perspective.

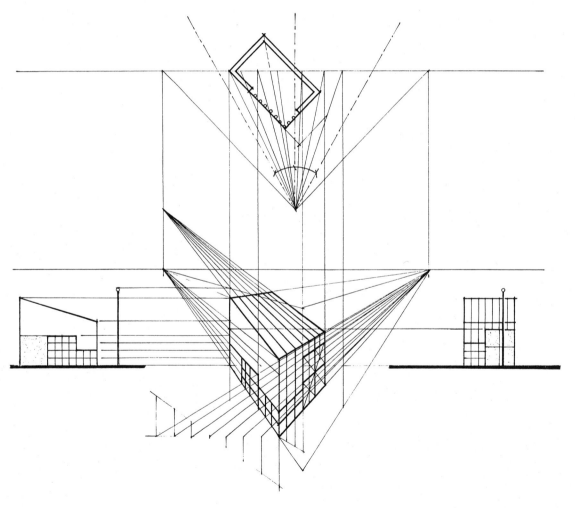

5-10. The finished projection.

Step 2: Tentatively locate the plan and elevation on your board (as shown) at the greatest possible distance apart, and tape them in place. This leaves the room for the completed projection in the center of the board. Tilt the plan at an angle so two façades will be viewed from the station point, SP.

Step 3: Place a sheet of cheap tracing paper over the plan and elevations. Use a big piece. Let it cover the whole board, and tape it down at the corners.

Step 4: Locate the station point, SP (fig. 5-12). Using a 30/60-degree triangle and a red pencil, lay out a 30-degree angle on each side of the axis of vision. Objects inside of this combined 60-degree cone will be ac-

ceptable. Objects outside of this cone will be excessively distorted. If your cone does not fit, pull your station point away from the object. You can also adjust the SP left or right to make minor adjustments in the way you look at an object. For major adjustments, rotate the plan instead. Avoid placing the SP so the axis of vision runs through the lead

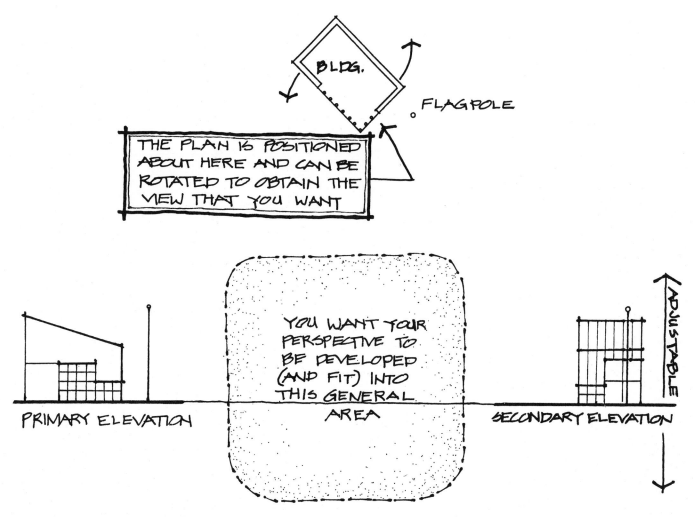

5-11. Steps 1, 2, and 3 of the mechanical perspective.

corner of the object. Although this is not critical, it allows a better view.

Step 5: Tentatively locate the picture plane (PP) through one of the corners of the object (building) in light pencil (fig. 5-13). If it works, darken the line with solid ink.

Step 6: With blue pencil, using dotted line, cast a 90-degree angle with the vertex at the SP and the legs parallel to the façades of the building. If the sides of this 90-degree angle intersect the picture plane somewhere off your board, reach under the yellow trash and rotate the building plan as necessary. Then try drawing a second 90-degree angle with the sides parallel to the newly positioned building façades.

Step 7: Locate the ground line on your elevation, extend it in solid ink, and label it GL.

Step 8: Locate and label the horizon line (HL) with a solid ink line. (This should be called the "eye" line, because it shows the position of your eyes.) If you want an aerial perspective, locate the line above the elevation drawing. If you want an eye-level per-

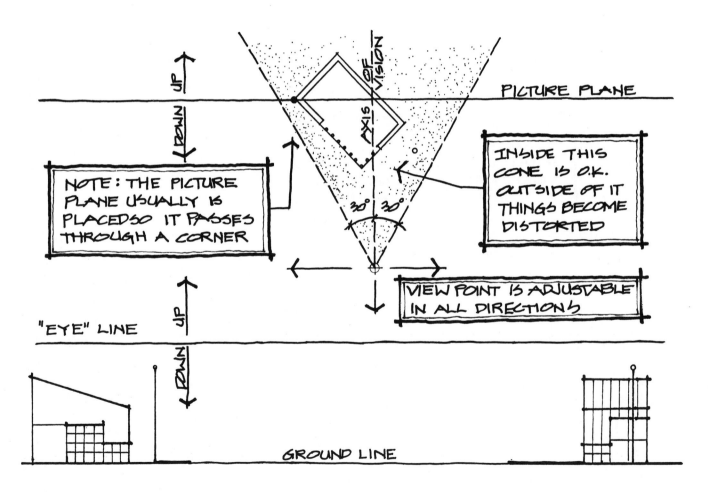

5-12. Step 4 of the mechanical perspective.

spective, locate the line at about five feet (in scale) above the ground line in your perspective. Obviously, we have opted for an aerial perspective in this example.

Step 9: Locate and label vanishing point left (VPL) and vanishing point right (VPR) by extending the dotted blue lines from the picture plane intersections down to the horizon line (HL) as shown. Circle VPL and VPR with a red pencil to make them easier to find.

Step 10: Extend and label the true height line (THL) with solid ink (fig. 5-14). Begin at the intersection of the PP and the corner of the building, and run it clear down past the ground line. (Note: In every case where a vertical height in the projection must be found, we begin at the elevation drawing, cast the height horizontally to the THL and manipulate it from there.)

Step 11: In light pencil locate the extreme right and left edge of the building. Draw a line from the station point through the extreme right and left corners of the building (in plan view) until it strikes the PP, then perpendicu-

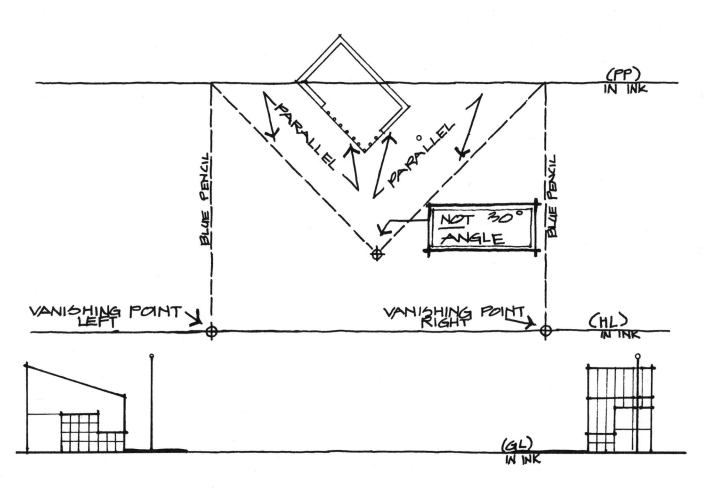

5-13. Steps 5, 6, 7, 8, and 9 of the mechanical perspective.

lar down through the projection zone. This may extend well past the GL. Note that in this example the THL happens to coincide with the left limit of the building.

Step 12: If the width of the projections looks all right, then similarly cast the other major corners of the building in light pencil. Remember, draw from the SP toward or through the corner, until the line reaches the PP, then down past the GL. Note: If one of the corners is beyond the PP, draw from the SP toward the corner until you reach the PP, then down past the GL. In all cases begin at the SP and turn at the PP. (Turning down at the corner itself, instead of the PP, is a common mistake.)

You have just set the horizontal location of the major corners of your building within the projection zone. The horizontal position of other minor points can be similarly set later, after you decide that you like the view you have selected.

Step 13: Turn your attention to the vertical heights of the corners. Begin at the elevation

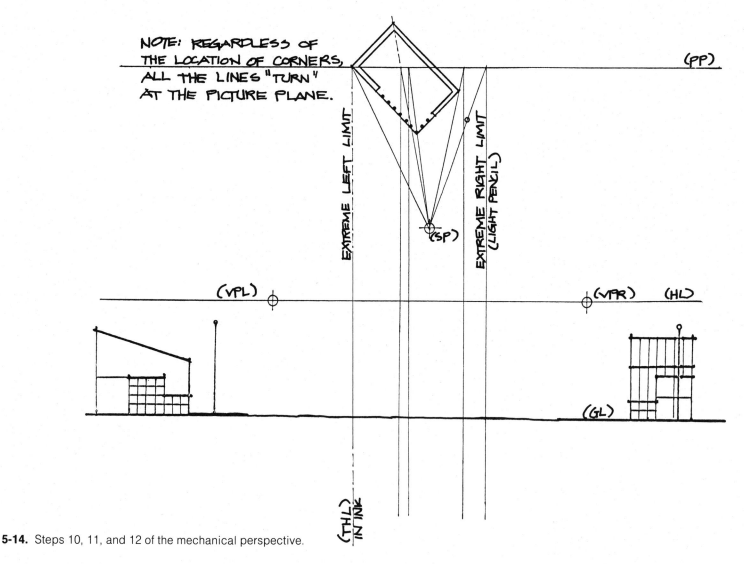

5-14. Steps 10, 11, and 12 of the mechanical perspective.

drawing (fig. 5-15). Transport the height of the top and bottom of one of the corners horizontally over to the THL. (Note that we will be repeating the process for the other corners and the flagpole.)

Step 14: Using VPL and the true height (at A), project the height out to the next corner (at B). Note that the height "grows" as it approaches the viewer. This is necessary and good, and makes a perspective look real. Let's call this the adjusted height.

Step 15: Notice that the back corner of the building happens to coincide with the THL. Notice also that the back corner (at A) is taller than the front. Set that taller height as before, then connect the corners to form the façade of the building. To make the façade clearly visible, darken in these object lines with dark pencil.

Step 16: Now for the front façade (fig. 5-16). Using VPR and the adjusted height at the front corner B, project light pencil lines past the other front corner, at C. Again darken in the object lines with dark pencil.

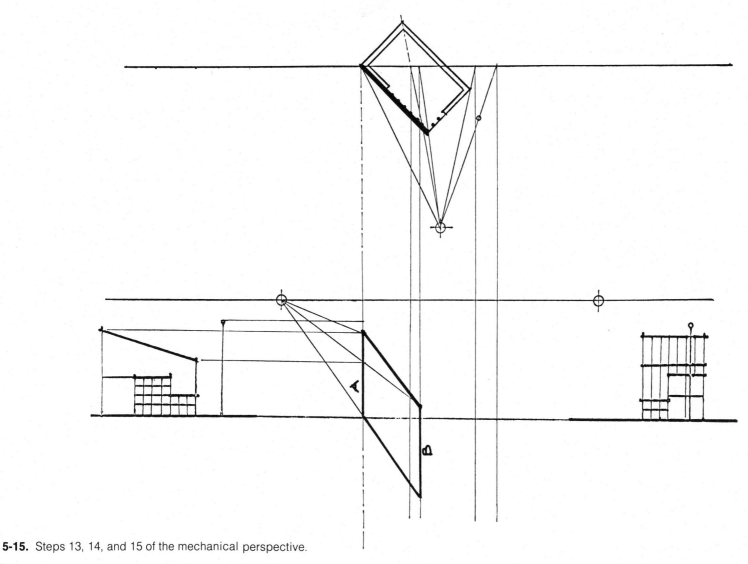

5-15. Steps 13, 14, and 15 of the mechanical perspective.

Step 17: The heights of the back corners can be similarly determined and the object lines darkened in (fig. 5-17).

To review what has been done so far:

The horizontal position of an object is set first. To do this, project a light line from the SP to or through the object until the line reaches the PP. Then drop the line from that intersection down past the GL. The horizontal position is now set.

Then set the vertical heights. Begin at the elevation drawing and transfer them to the THL. Using the vanishing points, project past the true height. In this way the adjusted vertical height is transferred to the previously set horizontal location. When you have enough points set, darken in the object lines.

Step 18: What happens if you want to include a tree, a flagpole (as in this case), or some other object that is not part of the building? Easy. Pretend that the flagpole is a corner on the building. Set its horizontal position

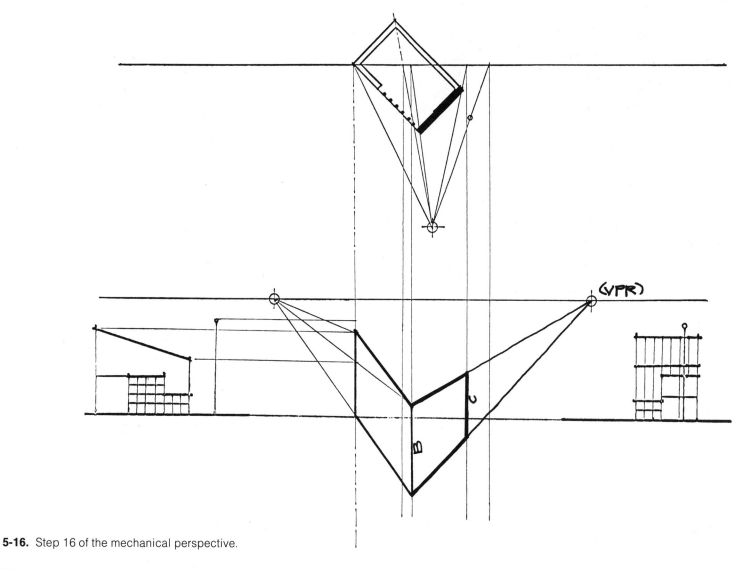

5-16. Step 16 of the mechanical perspective.

using the SP, plan, and PP, just as before (at D). Also set the vertical height just as before, using the elevation, the THL, and the vanishing points (fig. 5-18).

One additional trick must be used. You must create a false corner (at E). Essentially this enlarges the building so that the flagpole is on the front façade. Notice the adjusted height of the flagpole as it is carried through the imaginary corner at E.

Step 19: To include doors and windows, project the horizontal position of their edges just as before. Use the SP, plan, and PP, casting light pencil lines down past the façade on which they are located (fig. 5-19).

Pick up the head and sill heights of the window or head and base of the door opening from the elevation and transfer them to the THL. Using the vanishing points, project the adjusted height across the window edges on the façade, and darken in the window.

Step 20: To locate regularly spaced windows, we will generate a ghost measuring line as shown. Using any convenient scale on

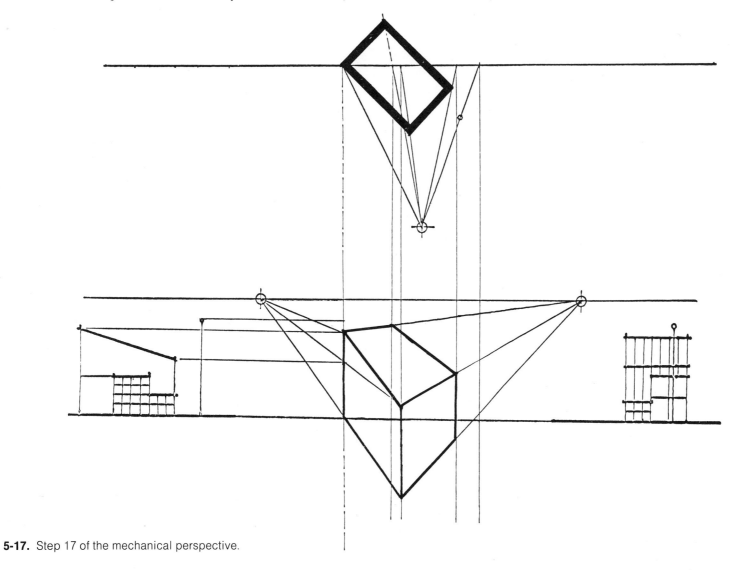

5-17. Step 17 of the mechanical perspective.

your architectural scale, divide the ghost measuring line into the appropriate number of divisions (seven in this example). Tilt the scale until the number of divisions matches the length of the ghost measuring line. Project the divisions from the scale to the ghost line.

Now project light pencil lines from the van-ishing point through the façade to each of the divisions on the ghost measuring line. Darken the window divisions. Vertical heights for the horizontal window mullions is trans-ported from the elevation, to the THL, to the façade by using the vanishing point, just as in all previous situations.

Step 21: The left side of the front façade has a similar window, and it is drawn in ex-actly the same manner, except that VPR was used to draw in the horizontal mullions.

A quicker way to divide the façade is to use the method of diagonals previously used for freehand perspectives.

Step 22: To complete the last step, we must recall that all parallel lines on any given

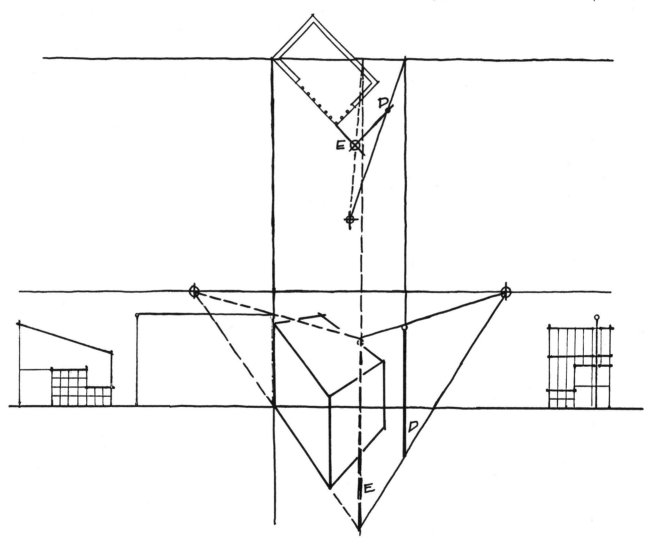

5-18. Step 18 of the mechanical perspective.

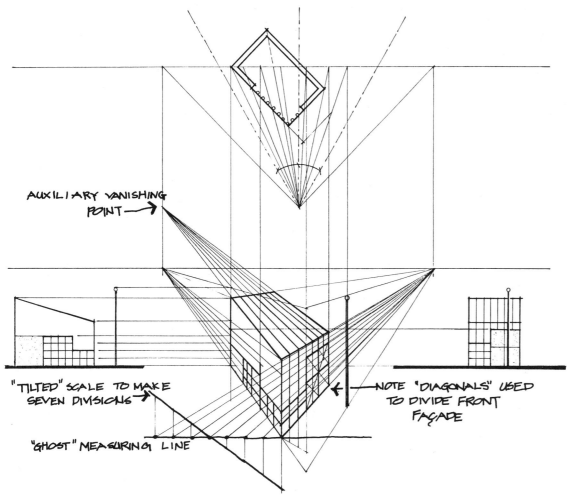

AUXILIARY VANISHING POINT →

"TILTED" SCALE TO MAKE SEVEN DIVISIONS →

"GHOST" MEASURING LINE

← NOTE "DIAGONALS" USED TO DIVIDE FRONT FAÇADE

5-19. Steps 19, 20, 21, and 22 of the mechanical perspective.

plane vanish at the same point. A different set of parallel lines on a different plane vanishes to a different vanishing point. For this reason we can project the edges of the roof until the two lines intersect. All of the parallel lines on the roof will vanish to this same point. Project light pencil lines across the roof from this auxiliary vanishing point. Darken those that are on the roof surface, and the perspective is complete.

Once it was necessary to redraw a perspective completely if the finished projection was not the right size. With enlarging and reducing photocopiers, this is no longer necessary.

If you would like to explore this critical skill further, try Claudius Coulin's *Step-by-Step Perspective Drawing* or Robert Duncan's *Architectural Graphics and Communications.*

ENTOURAGE **6**

Before we begin, draw your best scale figure. How good is it? Set it aside.

You cannot learn to draw entourage the night before a presentation. How long does it really take? One weekend. That's right, just one weekend—if you have the right attitude, the right standards, and the right system.

Before you set pencil to paper, you must have a confident attitude. Those who feel professional results are beyond them have no hope of achieving professional results. And you must maintain quality standards: compare your drawings only to the best professional work you can find. Finally, drawing entourage requires a system. You are not painting portraits here, you are merely adding graphic elements to embellish your rendering. Foolishness makes a designer want to invent his own entourage. Steal and copy. Published clip books make it easy (see the bibliography for examples). The following technique will help you improve your entourage drawing skills. Although people are the subject in the instructions, this technique can be used to perfect the drawing of any entourage.

Begin with the Sunday newspaper. Drawings of "beautiful" people are found in the advertisements for clothing stores. Find some that are 8 inches or taller and cut them out (fig. 6-1).

Step 1: Using your clipboard and typing paper, trace the drawing. This forces you to simplify faces, hands, and feet (fig. 6-2).

Step 2: Your tracing will be a simplified version of the original, but is it just as excellent? No. Retrace until it is. Now, if you had to, you could trace it into a presentation.

Step 3: Next, place the original illustration right beside your clipboard and parallel-draw the same figure at the same size (fig. 6-3). Keep trying until it is as good as the original. You will do better than you think be-

6-1. Sample drawing of beautiful person. (Arrow shirt ad, courtesy of Skay McCall, McCall's Store for Men and Ladies, Norman, OK.)

cause of what you learned in doing the earlier tracings. Now you can use the figure on opaque presentation boards.

Step 4: Once your parallel drawing looks perfect, try changing the size while parallel-drawing the same figure.

Notice that, as you make the figure smaller and smaller, less and less of the detail can be included. Facial features are lost altogether. Outlines assume an exaggerated importance. If your drawing continues to look excellent in this reduced and simplified condition, you can now use the figure as a "distant" figure in a perspective drawing.

Try making the figure larger and larger. Abandon the clipboard, as it will limit the size too much. Progressively increase the drawing size to 18 by 24 inches. This is more difficult, because you will need to add detail that is not in the original drawing. Get a friend to pose for you. Look at your model only for the additional detail that you need to complete your enlarged drawing. You are really learning where the important lines are. Once you have practiced enough, you will be able to adjust the size of the figure to suit your needs for a specific presentation.

Step 5: Try drawing the same figure from memory. Compare it closely to the original. It probably is not quite as good. Study the details of the original closely and practice until your memory drawing is perfect. You now have a scale figure for use anywhere, anytime. (But only one.)

Step 6: Repeat the preceding steps for several scale figures. Practice until they are all perfect. Notice that the critical lines shift around in the various figures because of their body posture and positioning. Each additional figure teaches you something useful in drawing all figures. Observe this well.

Step 7: Set two different original figures adjacent to your clipboard. Parallel-draw one of them, but modify its body position to match that of the second figure. After this becomes easy, ask your friend to model for you again. This time draw directly and completely from life. Compare the first drawing you did before reading this technique with your last drawing. It was a good weekend.

6-2. Trace the cutout.

6-3. Parallel-draw the cutout.

ELEGANT FIGURES

Most clients do not want to see themselves as odd character actors. Those clever devils who made those advertisements you have been using are well aware of the way clients want to see themselves. With few exceptions, fill your drawings with "beautiful people" with whom your client can empathize (fig. 6-4).

Elegant figures are elongated. Use longer legs, attractive faces, and the right clothes. Be sure to focus the attention of these elegant figures on the best part of your design. The figures should complement and explain the design, not steal the show.

Become an observer of people. Take photographs of crowds of diverse people. Try to put diverse people engaged in relevant activities into your presentations (fig. 6-5). If you have difficulty, look at *The Sketch* by Robert Oliver.

6-4. Elegant figure.

6-5. Include diverse individuals in your entourage.

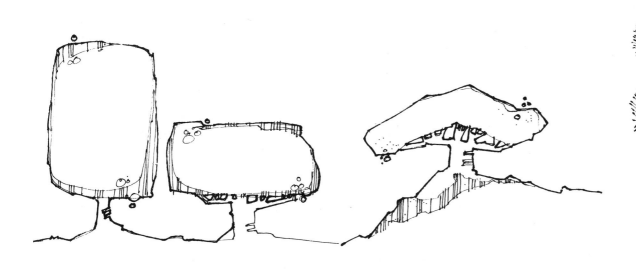

PLANT MATERIALS
Trees

A good reference for drawing trees is *Plan and Section Drawing* by Thomas Wang. Another excellent book is *Graphic Details for Architects* by Carl Kemmerich. The styles used in these books produce compatible, powerful line drawings.

Whatever style you choose, be certain that you have an adequate "vocabulary" of deciduous and evergreen trees (fig. 6-6). Make certain that they are compatible and that you have examples in plan, section, elevation, and perspective views (fig 6-7).

6-6. Deciduous and evergreen trees.

6-7. Trees in plan view.

Shrubs

Rely once again on Kemmerich and Wang for shrubs. Your "vocabulary" must include all views, as well as both deciduous and evergreen shrubs (figs. 6-8 and 6-9). Line drawings are best, because they will be easy to color if that becomes necessary.

Ground Covers

Ground covers are usually built up from various textures (fig. 6-10). William Kirby Lockard includes an excellent discussion of ground covers in *Design Drawing Experiences.*

Interior Plants

Broad leaves are common to plants that are used inside buildings (fig. 6-11). A wide variety of planters have also become available. It is advisable to choose one that will be available to your client.

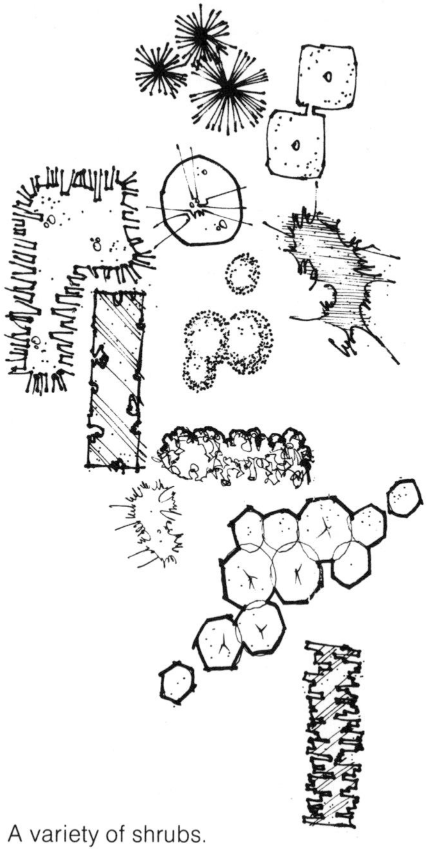

6-8. A variety of shrubs.

6-9. Shrubs completed in line drawings.

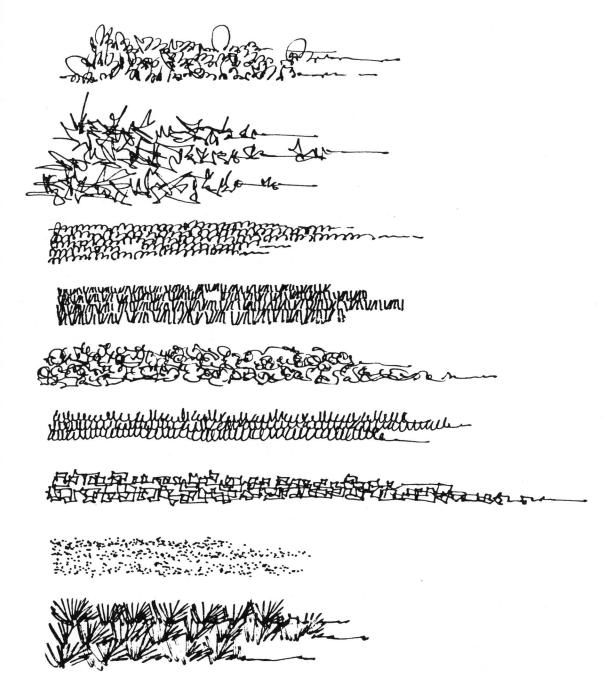

6-10. Ground covers.

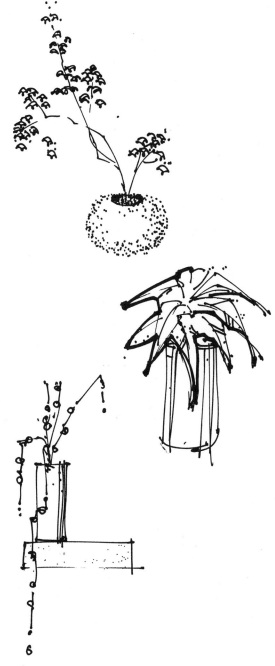

6-11. Interior plants.

VEHICLES
Automobiles

Cars are very often used as entourage. Be certain that you can draw them from any view and at every distance (fig. 6-12). Do not make them too beautiful, powerful, or extreme in any way or they may become more interesting than your design and distract your client's attention.

It is important to develop some variety in large groups of cars as in parking lots (fig. 6-13). A good source is new-car brochures. Spend a pleasant evening at the different car lots and let the sales personnel load you down with useful material.

Other Vehicles

Obvious choices for other vehicular entourage include trucks, airplanes, boats, and buses (fig. 6-14). Do not forget wheelchairs and baby carriages, which are often necessary to show specialized functions, such as handicapped access, in a design.

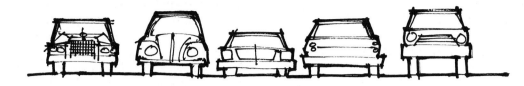

6-13. Include a variety of cars.

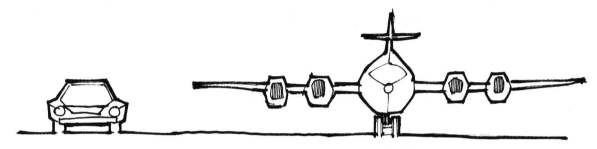

6-14. Other common vehicles.

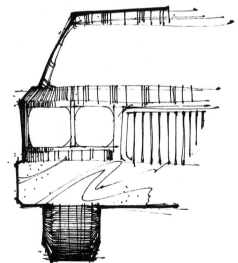

6-12. Automobile at a near distance.

FURNITURE
Interior Furniture

Many excellent tracing files are listed in the bibliography. However, it may be better to try going to the best furniture store in your area. If your client likes the presentation, there is a real possibility that he will try to have it built as drawn. Why dream up furniture that your client will not be able to find? You may also have a problem with selection and grouping of the furniture if it is taken from a tracing file. This will not be the case at the right store. Neither will the furniture be out of fashion.

Do not overlook the lesser pieces, such as lamps, magazines, books, ceramics, paintings, radios, and televisions (fig. 6-15). They make a space human. It is also a common mistake to overlook the less glamorous furniture.

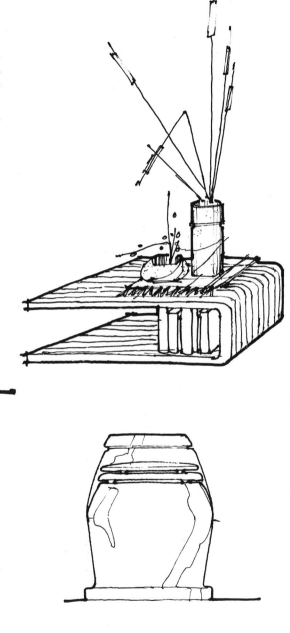

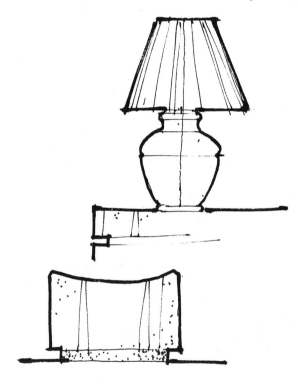

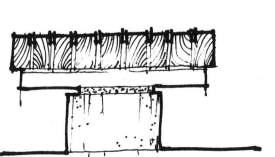

6-15. Indoor furnishings.

Exterior Furniture

A designer's repertoire should include a broad range of street furniture such as street lights, waste receptacles, benches, and bicycle racks. It is often necessary to resort to catalogs and current magazines to draw exterior furniture (fig. 6-16). Often they are not added as entourage to enrich a drawing but are instead important components that you have uniquely designed. In this case, no problem is encountered—just draw them as you designed them.

CONSTRUCTION MATERIALS

Although technically not entourage, showing the actual construction materials in your design requires the same skills as drawing entourage. Many sources show the standard indications used in plans and sections (fig. 6-17). *Architectural Graphic Standards* by Charles Ramsey and Harold Sleeper is a popular source, as is *Building Construction Illustrated* by Frank Ching. These books, however, do not consider the rendering of materials in elevations and perspectives. Realistic results, using all of the common media, are discussed by Albert Halse in *Architectural Rendering.* If you are using pencil, see Ted Kautzky's book *Pencil Broadsides.* In ink line drawing, *A Graphic Vocabulary for Architectural Presentation* by Edward White is a respected source.

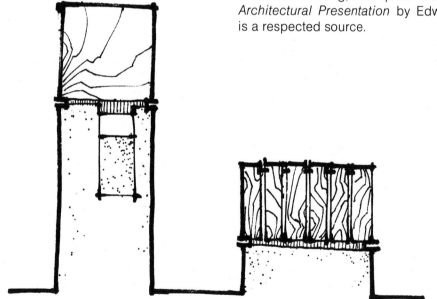

6-16. Exterior furniture.

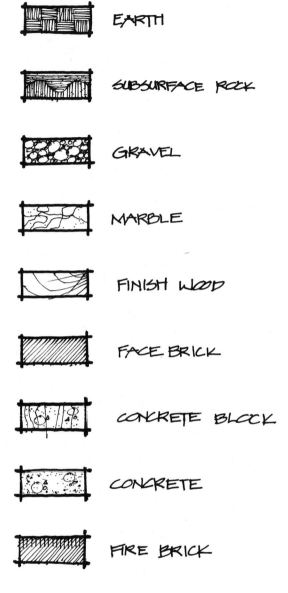

6-17. Construction materials.

When using any of these sources, it is helpful to remember hierarchy of line (fig 6-18). The darkest line is the outline of the total assemblage. The next darkest is the outline of each unit (brick, board, or stone). The lightest will be indications of surface textures and irregularities within each unit.

The most common difficulty arises in rendering reflective materials. It is a recognized practice to black in small windows completely (fig. 6-19) and leave large windows transparent. Some designers use adhesive pattern sheets (Zipatone, Formatt, and Letraset are popular brands) in either case (fig. 6-20). This technique is especially appropriate for buildings with flush-mounted glass.

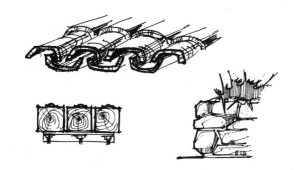

6-18. Remember hierarchy of lines.

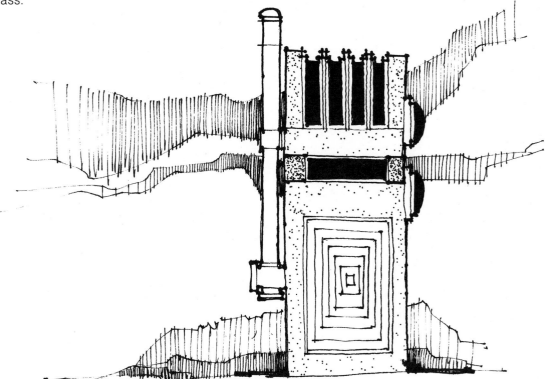

6-20. Adhesive pattern films make excellent windows.

6-19. Blacken in small glass areas.

One lesser known alternative is available for buildings that have medium-sized windows that are not surface mounted (fig. 6-21). Glass that is illuminated by direct sun is left brilliant white, while glass that is shaded is made completely black. The resulting drawings are very dramatic and reveal the depth of the window openings.

TRACING FILES

No chapter on entourage would be complete without a final reference to the excellent tracing files and clipbooks that are now available. Take a quick look at those listed in the bibliography the next time you are at the bookstore. Their use can put an immediate end to the outrageously poor entourage that ruins the presentation of many fine designs.

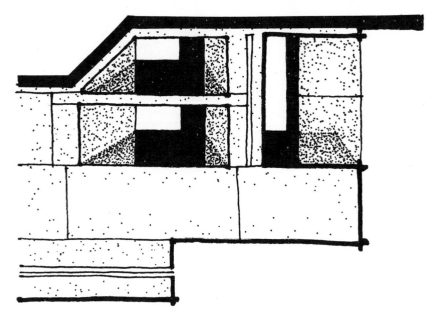

6-21. Shadows on recessed windows.

MEDIA 7

An astonishing variety of media is available to the designer. Whole books are devoted to each of them. Only a few of the easiest to use and most popular media will be discussed in this chapter.

GRAPHITE PENCIL

A design in which subtle tonal variation, textures, and the effects of light are important invites a pencil rendering. Pencil is fairly rapid and can be erased. The great master of pencil was Theodore Kautzky. Pencil rendering is not an easy method to learn, but it is possible by using the technique outlined in chapter 6 for drawing entourage. Retain very bright whites and bold, crisp darks for the best results.

Simple pencil line drawings, without shading and the like, are much more common and easier to produce. (fig. 7-1). Subtle variations can also be achieved with pencil (fig. 7-2). If a design is sufficiently rich in surface texture and detail, pencil line drawing is an adequate technique. A clear hierarchy of lines is critical. Using contour line technique will enable you to make the lines expressive and compelling. This is the best medium if a Diazochrome print is to be made for subsequent coloring.

Graphite pencil drawings can also be directly colored with colored pencils with adequate results (see fig. C-1 in the color insert). If a great deal of color is important to the design, graphite pencil is probably not the best choice.

With restraint, colored markers can also be used with graphite pencils.

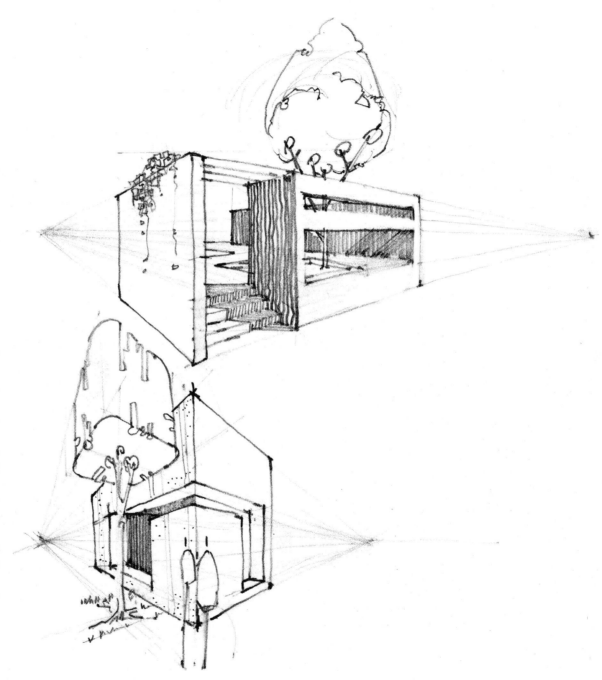

7-1. Pencil line drawings.

7-2. Note the subtle variations in the sky.

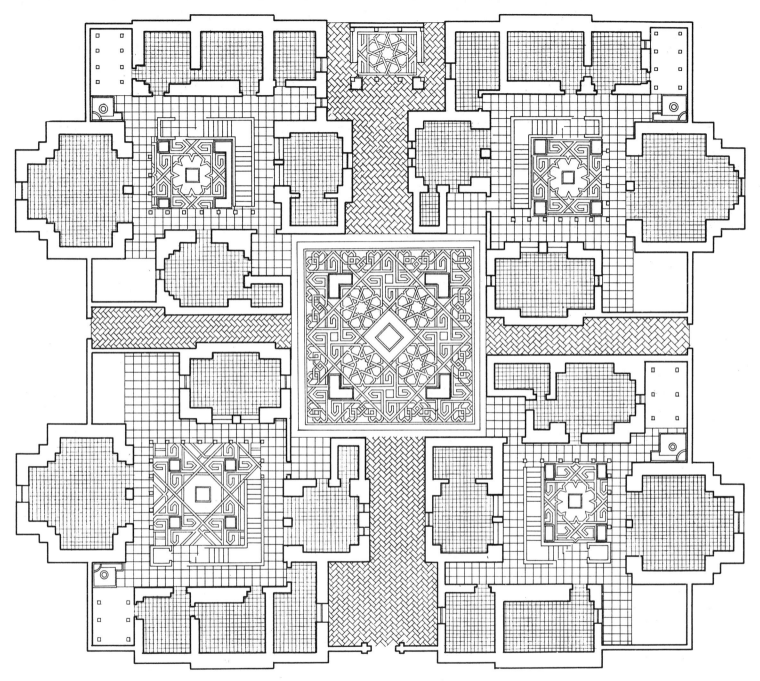

7-3. Technical pen drawing. (Student project by Randa Nadim Masri, University of Oklahoma: competition entry for a rural town in Egypt. Blueline print, 18- by 24-inch Mylar.)

INK

Avoid using technical pens if possible. If you cannot, look at Helmut Jacoby's books (see the bibliography) for examples and assistance. Technical pens are best for drawings intended for publication reproduction. They are appropriate in drawings requiring considerable detail and accuracy (fig. 7-3) Unfortunately, they are slow and difficult to use.

If possible, use the Flair and Razor Point pens instead (fig. 7-4). Do not try to use them with vellum drafting paper, however, or they will smear. If a print is to be run for subsequent coloring, use cheap canary or bum wad tracing paper in its place. Direct coloring on these papers can also be done with

excellent results. These drawings must be bold and decisive. Draw them freehand. William Kirby Lockard and Thomas Wang have excellent texts to guide you (see the bibliography). If color is to be included in the final rendering, this is the best medium for the initial line drawing. Then a combination of felt-tip markers and colored pencils is applied. The color can be applied on the face or reverse side of the paper (see fig. C-2 in the color insert).

COLORED PENCILS

It is possible, but unusual, to use colored pencils alone in a drawing. They resemble graphite pencils in that they can be used for

line drawings, but they are a poor choice if strong values and intense chroma are desired. If time is short, do not use them on very large drawings.

It is more common to use colored pencils to add a little quick color to a previously completed graphite pencil or ink line drawing (see figs. C-3, C-4, and C-5 in the color insert). Washes of colored pencil are gradually built up over such a drawing. Use the side, not the point, of the pencil, and a light circular motion. More intense washes are the result of more circles, not more pressure. Stronger results are possible by photographing colored pencil drawings on a light table. The effect is a bit like stained glass.

Working with colored pencil is not as fast as some novices imply, but erasure is possible. For speed and elegant results work small, then take slides of the drawing and project them during the presentation to the client.

FELT-TIP MARKERS

Like colored pencils, felt-tip markers are seldom used alone. The easiest technique involves applying light, transparent washes of grays over Diazochrome prints of good ink line drawings. Then "flavor" the grays with equally light colored pencil washes (see fig. C-6 in the color insert). Michael Doyle has emerged as the master of felt-tips. His book, *Color Drawing,* is particularly helpful with this subtle technique.

A second, more flamboyant style can also be used (see fig. C-7 in the color insert). Stronger, darker, less transparent felt-tip colors are applied over the Diazochrome prints. Less detail is required in the original ink line drawing, since the felt-tips will obscure it anyway. White or cream Prismacolor pencils are used with conical points to "lift" various

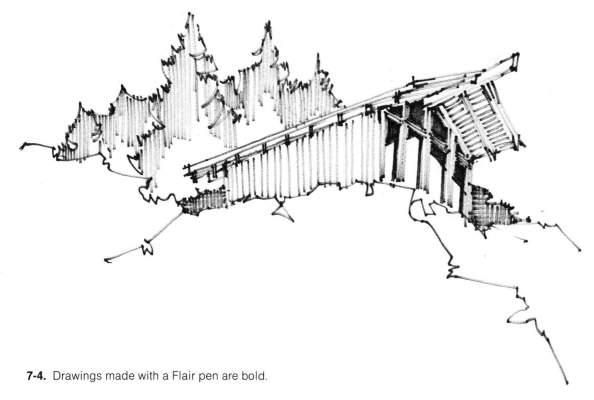

7-4. Drawings made with a Flair pen are bold.

objects (such as trees) above other surfaces. A sparkling drawing should be the result. Special attention must be paid to exploiting the white of the paper. Mike Lin of Kansas State University has taught large numbers of designers to use this technique. Shadows are created easily by adding a second wash of the same marker after the first wash has dried.

Conventional broad-point felt-tip markers are not a good choice for small, detailed drawings. The Mars Staedtler marker includes a sharply pointed brush that makes detailed work much easier and works well with pencil.

PASTELS

Although currently out of fashion, pastels are an excellent quick medium for colored renderings. Direct drawing is used for large, rapid color studies (see fig. C-8 in the color insert). Do not draw *lines* with the tips; in-

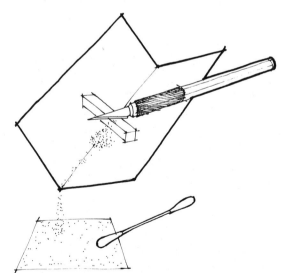

7-5. Washes of pastel are easily made by powdering the pastel with a knife and using a cotton swab.

stead, draw *surfaces* with the sides or edges of the chalk. Work big. Do not expect strong values, sharp dramatic lines, or intense colors.

It is possible to shave a colored "powder" off a pastel stick using a small sharp knife (fig. 7-5). Powder from the various sticks can be mixed together in the fold of a piece of paper, sprinkled into an area of a good line drawing, and rubbed into the surface with a cotton swab or a small cotton ball. Do not worry about staying inside the lines. Just use an eraser and an eraser shield once the light transparent wash has been applied. Albert Halse gives excellent guidance on this and other techniques in his book *Architectural Rendering.*

WATERCOLOR

This is the "top of the line" in formal renderings. Unfortunately, very few designers have sufficient skill to exploit this versatile medium. Great detail and subtle color are possible with watercolor. Albert Halse is the best author to read if you are interested.

One simple method is easily within reach of designers but has not been used a great deal since the development of felt-tip markers (fig. 7-6). Complete a good waterproof ink line drawing on a piece of white watercolor board. Using masking tape, tape all four edges to mask off a suitable frame for the drawing. Mix a very small amount of beige and yellow watercolor with water in a small watercolor dish. Using a broad 2-inch brush, wet the total drawing area inside of the taped frame with clear water. (A sponge will also work.) The surface should be uniformly damp. Now apply an even but very faint wash of the beige/yellow to the dampened area, using the 2-inch brush. Set the drawing flat, allow it to dry, and remove the tape. The result is so

faint that it can only be seen in comparison to the bright, white outer frame. This wash will mute the intensity of any other colors that you choose to add to the drawing. Buy some Frisket masking paper or Maskoid masking liquid. Complete the rendering by masking all areas except that to be colored, then applying a very transparent wash of your chosen color. After the area is dry, mask it, unmask the next area, and continue. Small areas can be washed with the right brush without masking. You can also draw directly with a watercolor brush.

Often a monochromatic scheme is used, and only one area is colored. With watercolor it is easier to control the result than with felt-tip markers, and the watercolor wash does not add any additional unwanted texture to the line drawing. Watercolor also will not obscure detail, and subtle hues of any type may be mixed. When the newness wears off, many will abandon felt-tips for this remarkably easy and elegant technique. Most designers prefer to prepare a small rendering and then take slides of it for the presentation.

AIRBRUSH

The most unique capability of the airbrush is the production of a graded wash (fig. 7-7). Most beginners can easily execute this simple technique, which can be used to make a simple but powerful sky. Mask all areas except that to be sprayed, just as you would for watercolor. You can also make your own tracing paper mask and lightly tape it in place. Follow the manufacturer's instructions for using the airbrush. Make the sky dark at the top and light at the bottom.

Similar results are possible by lightly dipping the bristles of a toothbrush into ink, then raking the bristles with your thumb to splatter the masked "sky" area.

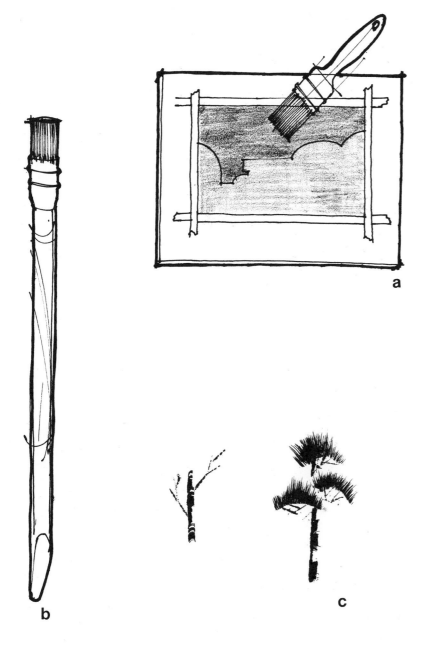

7-6. *a.* Watercolor washes are faster than markers in some cases. *b.* Watercolor brush. *c.* Direct brushwork tree trunks.

7-7. Graded wash with an airbrush.

ADHESIVE SHADING FILMS AND LETTERING

These are rapid (but expensive) ways to enrich a drawing (fig. 7-8). These materials are sold under the brand names Zipatone, Formatt, and Letraset, among others. They are available in a wide variety of screens and patterns. You simply choose the pattern you want, remove the backing, lay it onto the drawing, cut away the pattern from where you do not want it, and burnish the remaining pattern in place. They come in limited sheet sizes, so you should not plan on covering large areas without unsightly seams.

You can do your own freehand lettering for letters that are up to about ¼ inch high, on a single line. For larger letters or longer copy, use dry-transfer lettering or stencils, for neatness.

MODELS

Models are small-scale mockups of the actual design. They are usually the best means available for explaining the three-dimensional exterior appearance of a building.

Start with a ½-inch rigid insulation board as a base. Most designers cut it to a 24- by 36-inch rectangle with a very sharp carpet knife. Then stretch a piece of fine-woven cloth over the insulation and pin the edges in place. Warm gray or beige is the best color. Finally construct a frame for the base from one-by-two-inch pine and finish the edges with the molding of your choice. You are now ready to begin the model (fig. 7-9).

Cut the site, or area to be studied, out of mat board or particleboard. Build up the contours using this same material (fig. 7-10).

Mask off areas not to be grassed, and then paint the unmasked grass areas with a cheap flat enamel in a drab green. While the area is still wet, generously sprinkle an abundance of flock (of the same drab green color) onto the painted area. Tap the bottom of the board to make the flock scatter and uniformly cover the paint. After the paint dries, blow off the excess. The result is very realistic (fig. 7-11). Flock is available at arts and crafts stores and at model railroad stores. While you are there, buy bags of very finely ground cork, sand, and drab green sponge. Now you have stone and bark mulch and ground cover plants. Apply all of these in the same way.

Concrete walks and walls are made from warm gray #2 mat board (fig. 7-12).

Balsa wood is best for wooden surfaces (fig. 7-13). Steel is often represented with mat board or thin plastic sheets. Exposed aggregate concrete is best made from fine sandpaper.

For glass and water, use gray Plexiglas (fig. 7-14). Lightpoles are made with map pushpins with white heads (fig. 7-15). Once you know the scale of your model, you can add toy cars and trucks; paint them flat black.

Deciduous trees are made from a weed called yarrow (fig. 7-16). Some stores that sell materials for dry flower arrangements carry it. Shrubs are available in great diversity if you cut the heads off of various types of weeds. Colorful flower beds can be made with very very small beads.

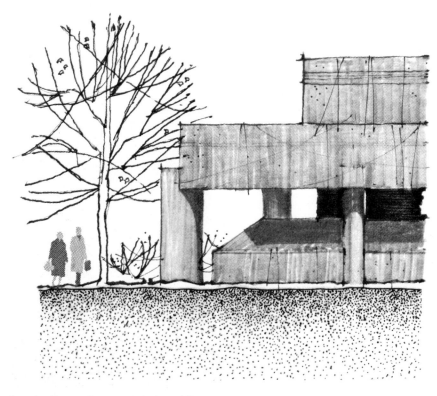

7-8. Adhesive shading patterns can be used to improve a simple drawing quickly.

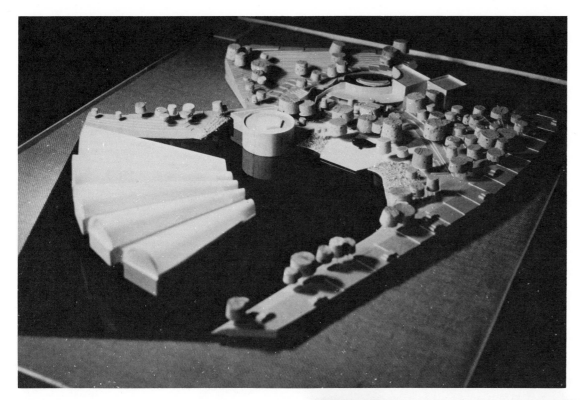

7-9. Note the model's cloth-covered base. (Student design by Pat Schoenfeldt, University of Oklahoma: Oklahoma City Zoo Project. 24- by 36- inch model.)

7-10. Topographic contour study model. (W. C. Muchow Associates, Denver, CO: University of Colorado Events Center, Boulder, CO. 18- by 24- inch base.)

7-11. Note the flocking used to simulate grass. (Student design by Mark Gandy, University of Oklahoma: urban plaza. 12- by 18-inch model.)

7-12. Note the "concrete" walls. (Student design by Stuart Copedge, University of Oklahoma: urban street. 24- by 36-inch model.)

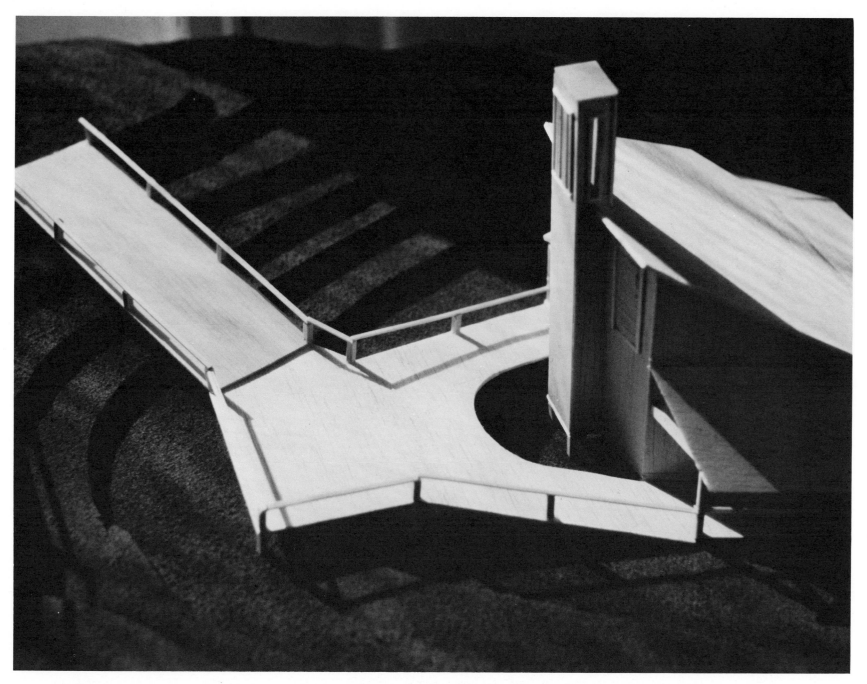

7-13. Note the wooden surfaces created with balsa wood. (Student design by Mike Foley, University of Oklahoma: chapel. 18- by 24-inch model.)

7-14. Note the use of Plexiglas for water. (Student design by Pat Schoenfeldt, University of Oklahoma. 18- by 24-inch model.)

7-15. White pushpins are used for streetlights. (Student design by Andres Elias, University of Oklahoma. 18- by 24-inch model.)

7-16. Use yarrow for trees. (Student design by Keith King, University of Oklahoma: shared residential open space. 18- by 24-inch model.)

Your model may be schematic, showing only circulation, land use, and general massing (fig. 7-17), conceptual, only investigating an idea (fig. 7-18), or realistic (fig. 7-19).

When your model is finished, a Plexiglas cover can be made to protect it. You will need adhesive tape, acetone, a hypodermic syringe, and a lot of practice. Go to a nearby glass store that sells Plexiglas and ask for help. Practice adhering taped corners with the acetone in the syringe. Buy some cheap scrap for this practice. Be careful with the acetone, as it can be deadly.

When photographing your model, use the same warm gray cloth you bought to cover your base as a background. Use pins, not glue, to attach your model to the base. This way the base is reusable.

Sanford Hohauser's book is the best to read for more information about architectural models (see the bibliography).

7-17. Schematic model. (Student design by M. Wahl, University of Colorado: multiuse urban redevelopment area. 4- by 8-foot base.)

7-18. Conceptual study model. (18- by 24-inch base.)

7-19. Realistic model. (Student design by Mark Wainscott, University of Oklahoma: multiuse high rise. 24- by 36-inch base.)

C-1. Graphite- and colored-pencil drawing.

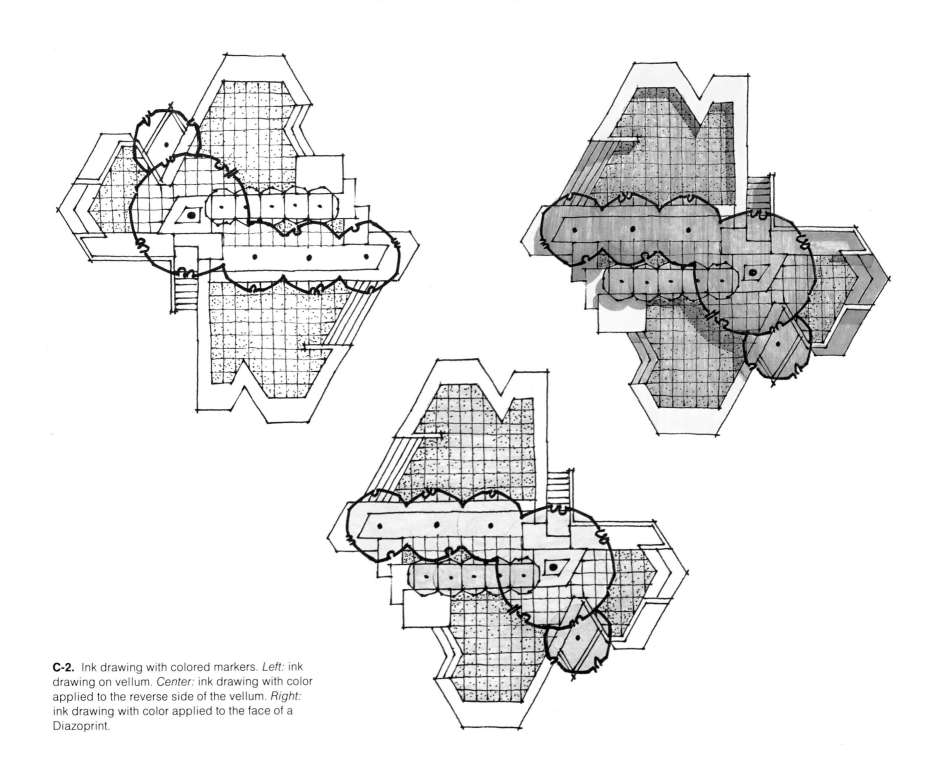

C-2. Ink drawing with colored markers. *Left:* ink drawing on vellum. *Center:* ink drawing with color applied to the reverse side of the vellum. *Right:* ink drawing with color applied to the face of a Diazoprint.

C-3. Graphite- and colored-pencil drawing.

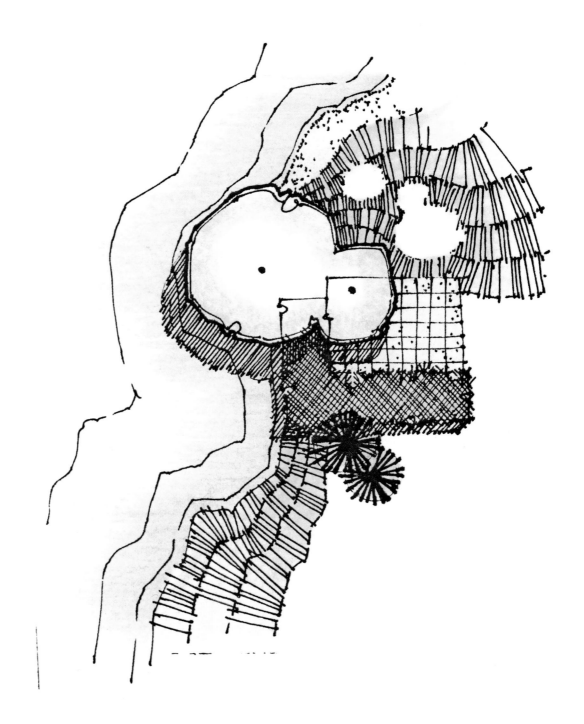

C-4 and C-5. Light colored-pencil shading on ink drawing. The muted colors here are achieved by lightly shading one ink drawing, more darkly shading a copy of the same drawing, and sandwiching the two together, light over dark.

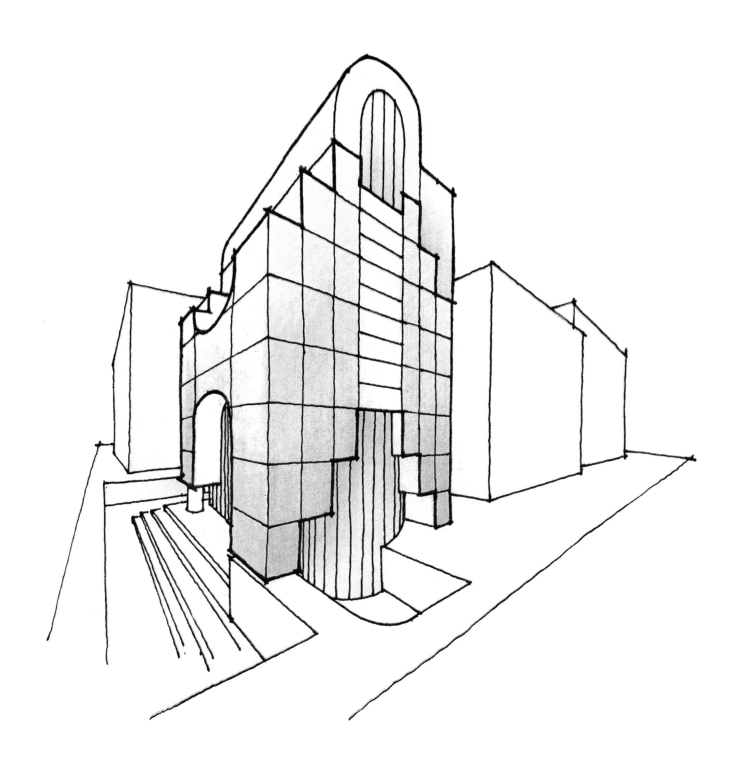

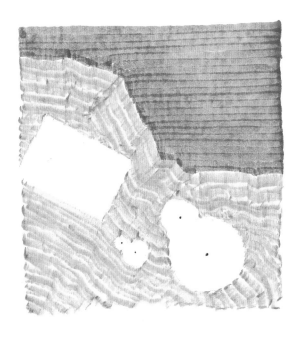

C-6. Gray-marker and colored-pencil drawing.

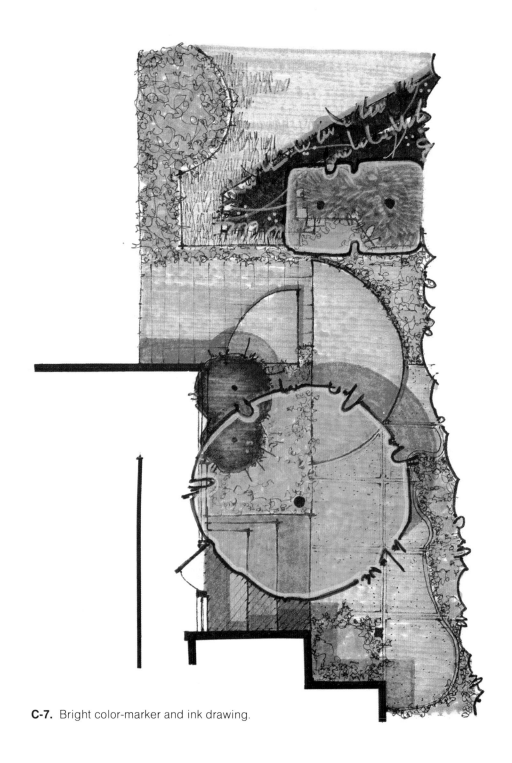

C-7. Bright color-marker and ink drawing.

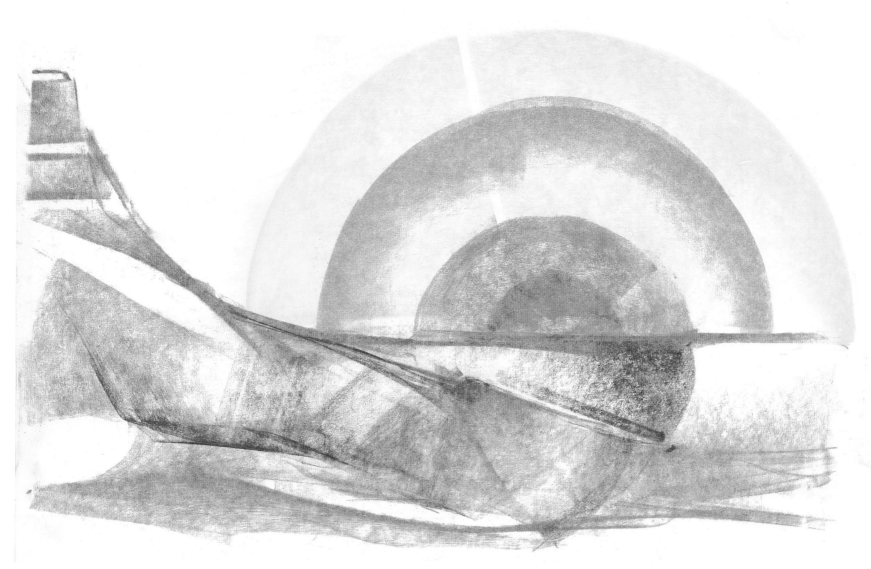

C-8. Direct drawing with pastels.

C-9. Hue scheme.

C-10. Chroma scheme.

EXHIBITS 8

All presentations have some elements of display. Work will be exhibited before, during, or after the actual verbal presentation. On occasion, a designer's work is shown without benefit of an accompanying verbal presentation. In such circumstances, much can be learned from the commercial display designers used by department stores, conventions, and museums.

PRINCIPLES

The composition of exhibits and displays conforms to the same principles previously outlined in chapter 4; however, there are some standard arrangements that appear regularly. Elements in the display can be organized into pyramids (fig. 8-1), zigzag (fig. 8-2), spiral (fig. 8-3), stepped (fig. 8-4), circular (fig. 8-5), radial (fig. 8-6) or planar (fig. 8-7) arrangements.

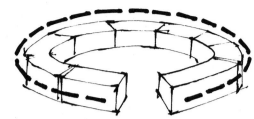

8-5. Circular display arrangement.

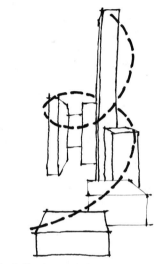

8-3. Spiral display arrangement.

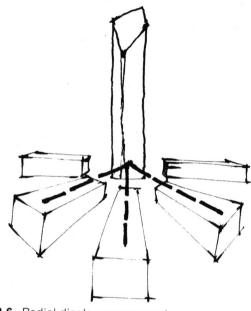

8-6. Radial display arrangement.

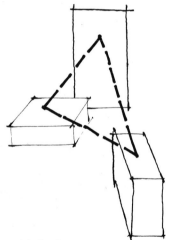

8-1. Pyramid display arrangement.

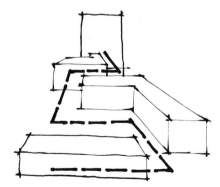

8-2. Zigzag display arrangement.

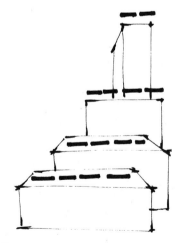

8-4. Stepped display arrangement.

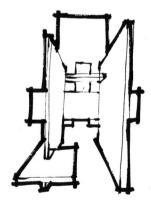

8-7. Planar display arrangement.

The materials should also be grouped into some easily recognizable order. Elements are often grouped by sequence, issue, or like content (fig. 8-8).

A central idea, slogan, theme, or concept should unify the exhibit. A slogan, if used, should be brief, simple, easy to recognize and understand, truthful, and persuasive.

Decide what is important, and establish a clear hierarchy of importance among the elements in the exhibit. Be certain the exhibit tells the client clearly what is critical. Use size, location, and lighting to make your intentions unmistakable (fig. 8-9).

Coordinate color to enliven and clarify your motives. Subordinate color to masses and spaces made by the arrangement of elements in the display. Also be certain that space and light collaborate with color to create unified results. Restrict strong contrast to drive home only the most important points.

Form powerful uninterrupted lines and suppress fussy detail. Keep the spaces bold and simple.

Make a clear decision between formal or informal balance and consistently apply the one you choose.

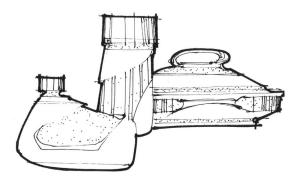

8-8. Group like items.

8-9. Make effective use of space and light.

DISPLAY PLANNING

Consider the type of material to be shown. Is it a three-dimensional model or a small two-dimensional drawing? Think about your client's values, interests, and appetites. How large is the display area, and what is its shape? Take a look at the available lighting and other technical facilities. Consider the time, talent, and money that can be invested in the display. Most important, keep the central goal or idea of the exhibit in mind.

Make a real plan for the exhibit. This includes circulation, lighting, and sound. Design the movement of viewers as a choreographer arranges the movements of dancers. Do not ignore the chaos caused by the colors of their clothes and the noise that they will make.

If brochures are to be made available, coordinate them with the rest of the exhibit.

Make drawings. Select the specific work to be shown, and begin their final preparation. This can include making protective covers for models, having drawings framed, and photographing selected work. Obtain or fabricate the necessary screens, partitions, and stands. Clean and prepare the exhibit area.

Do not forget maintenance and security during the exhibit. Include teardown and cleanup after the exhibit in your planning.

COORDINATE YOUR DISPLAY WITH YOUR PRESENTATION

The message of your display and of your presentation must be the same. If the display is to be used during the verbal presentation, adequate seating will have to be part of your planning. If a reception will be part of such a presentation, be certain that the design work on exhibit will be protected against damage by careless guests with refreshments.

VOCABULARY OF EXHIBITS

Merchandisers have devised a standard display vocabulary. Figure 8-10 shows the most common terms currently in use.

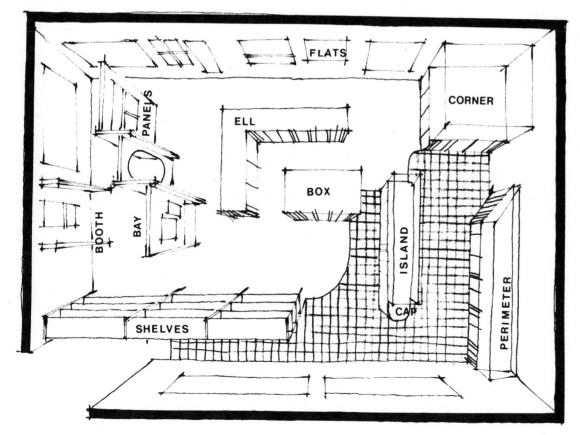

8-10. The vocabulary of displays.

PRESENTATION 9

Finally, the day of the actual face-to-face final presentation to the client arrives. You, your consultants, and your colleagues have worked long, intelligently, and imaginatively. All that remains is to confirm that your client is satisfied. At this point it becomes apparent that architects and designers are in a "people" business just as surely as they are in the "sticks and bricks" business. But remember, the presentation should not be an ordeal. It is certainly not like selling brushes door-to-door. The client wants to build something or he would not have approached you. This client has chosen *you* to do it. He has invested time, money, and confidence in you. You may be a bit nervous, but so is the client. He has a lot riding on you. He wants and needs for you to succeed. In short, he wants to say yes. The client has invested considerable trust in you up to this point. Today you reward him for that trust. When it is all done, he will not only have a fine building, interior, or landscape; he will also have this important day as part of his life.

IS SELLING A DIRTY WORD?

It can be, no argument. But it does not have to be, and *failure* to sell may be just as serious. Consider this. You believe in what you have done for the client. It will do a lot of good for a lot of people. You have diligently gotten to know your client and his real needs. Think for a moment of all the good things that he and the general public will lose if your project is never built. Consider the waste of time and talent if you fail to explain and demonstrate the good thinking that has been done on your client's behalf. You are not planning to ask the client to accept blindly some "pig-in-a-poke," are you? We all sell. Draftsmen, job captains, primary designers, principals, consultants, and clients all have different viewpoints. Their interests, backgrounds, and current needs are all different. It is only normal that they initially occupy different positions. Projects succeed because all involved are willing to discuss ideas. Each person acts in good faith and proposes what is best in his experience. The persuasion that exists between these parties is not immoral, it is essential. Projects improve because of it. This discussion or persuasion has another name that professionals do not like: selling.

GOALS OF A PRESENTATION

A good presentation will accomplish the following:

- Seize and hold the client's attention
- Clearly, completely, and convincingly explain the project
- Clearly satisfy the client's needs
- Get a "yes" answer or clarify objections
- Lead to action
- Make a friend

THE PLANNING PROCESS

Obviously, you are professionally competent; you have your license. However, the principal doing the presentation may or may not have executed the majority of work for the project. Questions have a habit of becoming uncomfortably detailed, and if you do not know the answers, your client may be less inclined to accept the project, regardless of why you do not know.

Often many individuals in a firm may be qualified to make the actual presentation. The following traits have been cited as common in successful salespeople:

- Not moody or subject to worry
- Self-confident and self-sufficient
- Aggressive and willing to assume responsibility
- Sociable
- Not self-conscious
- Not inclined to talk about himself
- Not resentful of discipline or criticism
- A little unconventional

Others can be in attendance, but reflect on your client as a human being. From whom would he like to hear? Has he developed a close working relationship or personal friendship with someone in the firm? Often a team of people must be available to explain the design fully and to field questions. Be certain that the people you select actually do become a real team.

The client's appetites and real motives are too often neglected. Know his abilities and limitations. This includes his most current financial capabilities, courage, and experience. But you have done your homework, so you will not be caught on this one. It would not hurt to review the background that you have prepared, however, just to be sure. In choosing an approach and predicting objections, it might be helpful to classify your client as follows: is he talkative, silent, a fast talker, deliberate, impulsive, vacillating, trusting, suspicious, or opinionated? Every project is supported with an astounding number of facts. Very few facts may be necessary for the initial presentation; however, the questions that follow may require a complete command of data bases relating to a specific isolated area.

All facts and data should be collected and made ready in simple, accessible form for the meeting.

Pick the right stage for your presentation. It should be beyond interruptions, suitably elegant, and adequately equipped. There is a "power" potential here that cannot be ignored. Whole books are written on dressing for power, designing your office for power, and gaining power in your words. The subject is a bit offensive; however, that does not justify ignorance of such matters. These subjects are currently of keen interest in the business world. You can bet at least some of those at the meeting are familiar with such matters. Burglary is a bit distasteful too, but those who design banks need to learn something about a burglar's methods. A more palatable body of reading is available about body and face language. In negotiation, people speak with their body postures and facial expressions as well as with words. Learn to communicate effectively with your look and gesture as well as your voice.

Sometimes, no matter how well you plan, the deck is stacked against you before you walk in the door. The outcome of a meeting is often sealed at the moment the participants are chosen and the invitations are sent. Next time you see a news interview on television, watch closely. Usually there will be three or four people on the panel with a viewpoint shared by the newspeople, and one person with a viewpoint that opposes them. Guess who loses? Professionals do not need to do this. We also do not need to be victims of it.

Make an Outline

Know what you are going to say. A written outline is critical in directing an orderly presentation. If you write everything out fully, the presentation will be unbearably dull and will not allow for interruptions for comments and questions. Conversely, if you just "wing it," even you will be surprised at what you say—and forget to say. An outline can pull you back on the track after a question leads a presentation far afield. Developing the outline makes you clarify your thinking, put the information into a logical order, and anticipate problems. One last benefit comes from having an outline. If you tend to be a little nervous, it can be a security blanket.

In preparing the outline, first write the single most critical idea, slogan, or concept behind the presentation. Why is your design unusual or valuable? Not HOW is it different, but WHY. Now that you can clearly identify what you think is critical, determine what your client will think is most critical. Review his needs and motives and select an appropriate appeal.

Next consider the length of the presentation. Most sources recommend holding the time to under an hour. If you have a complex presentation, it might go to an hour and a half, but it probably should not. Ninety minutes is the absolute maximum.

Now check the sequence and organization of your presentation. See that it flows logically from one point to the next and that it intensifies as you lead your clients to a "yes" response. The typical sequence will probably parallel the next few paragraphs in this chapter.

Anticipate objections. This is critical. Get others to help. Think of every probable concern that a client could raise against your design, and prepare a response for each objection.

Leave a little room for flexibility in your presentation. For instance, the client may raise a valid objection that will send you back to the drawing board. How will you handle that situation? Perhaps he will say he likes it and then be unwilling to take immediate action. What is your plan for that eventuality? What if you focused on one issue and it becomes obvious that he is much more concerned about something else?

Rehearse Your Presentation

A rehearsal is imperative. If possible, it should be a full dress rehearsal, on the actual "stage" where it will be delivered, with an audience present. This allows you to practice your choice of words, to be certain all of your visual aids are operating correctly, and that the sequence is logical. If others will aid you in your presentation, it will also allow them to practice coordinating their efforts with yours.

Last-minute Preparation

Make one last check of your equipment and materials and get your heart right. Be confident, enthusiastic, sincere, and willing to serve.

THE PRESENTATION
Introduction

Start the presentation with your client's name. This whole thing is being done for his benefit, and you would not want him to doubt it.

Introduce yourself and other parties to the discussion if they have not met.

While the purpose or goal of the presentation should be obvious, it would not hurt to clearly state it: "This presentation has been prepared to gain Mr. Johnson's approval for the design of his new bank." This helps establish your control of the discussion and starts the meeting with the expectation that the meeting will result in action.

A brief explanation should be made outlining the scope and sequence of the presentation for the audience. Not only will this let everyone know where they are going, but it will encourage the group to stay on course.

Seize Attention and Imagination

One sound sales source suggests the following techniques for attracting and holding an audience's attention:

- Pose an "unsolvable" question
- State a startling fact or viewpoint
- Make a physical show instead of words
- State an emphatic benefit:
  —something he wants
  —something you can definitely supply
  —something substantiated by your presentation
  —be specific

Intensify Interest

Continue to develop the client's interest once you have attracted it. Allow him to identify with your search for the solution. Ask questions. Involve him in the human drama, frustrations, excitement, and personalities committed in this search. Keep it short and not too technical. Gradually begin to unfold the benefits of your design solution as part of the triumph of this challenging mystery story. Intensify his sense of need for the benefits he has requested. At the same time reveal alternatives and false paths that occurred. Involve the client in your frustrations as you were forced to discard each of the alternatives for clearly stated reasons. Do not be afraid of a little show biz. Make your points clear, complete, convincing, confidence-building, and competition-eliminating.

Invite Questions

As your formal presentation draws to a close, decisively ask for your client's questions. Address the group as a whole. Smile genuinely. Do not lose inertia and excitement with an awkward silence at the close during which your client is supposed to guess that it might be all right to ask a question. Decisively asking for questions retains your control of the meeting and invites genuine questions instead of objections.

Resolve Objections

Do not be too surprised if your client does not jump up with a hammer in hand ready to build the project. Welcome his objections and seriously evaluate them. If he has the kind of money it takes to complete this project, he surely knows something. Even if his objection has no basis in fact, it reveals more useful information about his motives that will be useful in the negotiation. Evaluate the level of resistance that is being exerted, and measure your response appropriately.

If you must refer to facts or make promises in resolving objections, be right, specific, simple, and able to deliver. Respond in keeping with his motives, experience, and intelligence. Mix authority and diplomacy.

Smile and be courteous. Protect his ego the way you would like him to respect yours. Make it easy for him to abandon his opposition with dignity. Keep listening, really listening to what he is telling you. Be conscious of passive as well as active resistance. Look behind his words. Do not consider just *what* he's saying—determine *why* he is saying it. Have you overlooked some hidden motive? Perhaps he really does not have the ability or authority to approve the project.

Some common reasons for resistance include:

- The client is satisfied with the present situation
- He has insufficient information
- The design does not appeal to him
- He is unable to take advantage of it
- The use is not sufficiently immediate
- It conflicts with other goals, habits, or plans
- It generates inconvenience
- He is suffering from caution or indecision
- You picked the wrong motivation or appeal
- He has been antagonized
- You pushed too hard

Take notes when he speaks. This will show respect and will perhaps show you a pattern in his objections; it also buys time to think if you need it. If his objections prove to be valid, you will have a good record of changes that must be made. Remember the research you did on your client's usual methods of operation and personality traits. How does this current objection fit into that picture?

After weighing the motivation and degree of resistance embodied in an objection, choose a response. Here are some common responses to objections.

Let it pass: Ignore the objection. If he does not raise it a second time, it was not a real obstacle, or it was just an excuse. If he does raise it a second time, he will say it differently and you will understand the objection more clearly. It is necessary to distinguish between real concerns and excuses. A continuous string of excuses means you are wasting your time, and the problem has nothing to do with your design.

Directly deny it: This technique can seem rude or honest and responsive. Use it with care. It can quiet a concern or prematurely terminate the presentation.

Indirectly deny it: This response requires finesse, so that you do not seem to be hedging, but it allows the client a graceful retreat.

Exploit it: Turn his logic around and show him why the design resolves it: "That's exactly why this design will work for you." Make it a reason for action.

Convert it into a question: This aids the client in focusing his concern into a single specific question. Then answer it.

Meet it with facts: Simply, helpfully, and unemotionally refute the objection with your data. Be sure your facts are correct and in an easily understood form.

Allow a minor concession: If the point is not critical, give in. If he likes the design, he will want to contribute too—not just by putting money on the table but by adding his intelligence to this important discussion.

Accept it as a genuine shortcoming: Every design has shortcomings. Balance these with the strengths of the design. Allow the client to see the shortcoming in the context of the big picture. Get him to say what he *does* like.

Your attitude in responding to objections is more important than the techniques that you choose. Listen, be patient, stay helpful, be factual, and stay tactful. Do not let the discussion become a dispute. If this happens, win or lose, you lose. Design is the interface between conflicting interests. It takes two to argue, and the price of an apology may be too high for both parties.

Review chapter 1. Consider whether a client is raising an objection, or actually saying "yes." Are his questions moving the discussion closer to implementation? "I should wait"—he is just asking for a little reassurance. "How difficult is something like this to build?" "When could something like this be completed?" These are not objections. He is telling you "yes."

Getting Approval

The client wants to approve your design and probably will. Get him to actually say the word "yes" to small questions and issues early in the presentation. Keep giving him opportunities to say "yes" throughout the presentation. Know those "yes" symptoms. Go for final approval as soon as the client is ready. Plans are good. Presentation outlines are good. But if the client is ready to say "yes," let him. The client is often ready to say "yes" at the end of your formal presentation, right after you resolve a major objection, or after a moment of hesitation.

Do not be too shy to ask directly for approval. Take your time and do not press, but make a trial effort. Do not throw down the gauntlet in a single moment of truth. If the trial for overall approval fails, help him to list the things he likes and try for approval step by step until you have it all. At the worst, you will probably have approval for a good deal of the design and will clarify specifically what must be done to obtain the rest.

An important part of the final approval is a commitment to proceed with action. Actions make buildings, not words, and actions have time schedules. Establish a working schedule before you close.

Conclusions

The ending of a presentation is like playing pool. In pool, each individual shot is not any more important than the way you prepare yourself for the next shot. At the end of a successful presentation, everybody wins. Whether a designer has been given total approval or not, everybody wins. You should be certain that feeling is felt and celebrated. The client who leaves the table is a potential future client and an advocate for the profession.

He is justifiably proud of what he has accomplished and the way you have helped him. He is ready to forgive the small frustrations that inevitably arise during actual construction. He is a friend that has been well served. He knows it and he feels it.

PRESENTATION TOOLS AND TECHNIQUES
Visual Aids

Samples: The choice of brick, glass, carpet, and the like invite the use of samples. Limit the number that are used. Keep the printed information with the sample, and do not let it become a plaything for the client during the rest of your presentation. Exploit the samples' sensualism—let the client touch as well as see them.

Photographs: Use photographs that amplify what is being said. Be certain that they have happy people in them.

Films and videotapes: These offer strong appeal to the senses. They can be run repetitively by the client in the designer's absence, they can be used to reach large audiences, and they can exert positive control over the sequence of that part of a presentation. When drawings and models are used, there is a danger that the client's interest will wander uncontrolled from one drawing to another. There is the risk that the presentation will dissipate into chaos or lose its inertia, bogged down by some remote issue. With film or videotape, the sequence and the total package of information is assured without interruption.

Drawings and models: These aids serve as excellent vehicles for a complex and extended discussion. They help the client focus on and express his concerns. Never describe what the client can see for himself.

Manuals and brochures: If extensive information is needed to support a presentation, send written material to the client before the meeting, as it can excite and precondition a client for a presentation. In this way, the client will have time to study the data, and the material will not compete with you for the client's attention during the presentation.

Charts and graphs: Like drawings and models, these must be large enough to be seen by the audience. Moreover, they must be very simple and easily understood. One message, one chart, then get it out of sight.

Written proposals: If required, proposals should be sent prior to a presentation. If this is not possible, they should be given at the end of a presentation to avoid drowning the client in detail while you talk.

Some Words about Words

Words, when properly chosen and used, are powerful tools for the designer. Use them to say only those things that your drawings and models cannot. Spend them like money. Keep your talk brief, straightforward, simple, vivid, visual, and emotional.

Use powerful descriptions. Choose words that are uncompromising, definitive, and unqualified. Think of your project's best features. List them. Now list alternative words and descriptions for each feature. Keep your descriptives in human terms: "Don't sell trees, sell shade" or "Don't sell a house, sell family shelter." Choose your most vivid, sharp, and electric words. Practice them. Use them in your daily life until they come naturally. For example, compare "I think this could be a nice space in a concrete building" with "A pool of light carved from structural concrete." It is normal to be uncomfortable with powerful words at first. Remember, it took time to learn to draw too. Powerful words sound foolish in trivial situations. A design is not a trivial undertaking, and it does not deserve trivial treatment.

How you phrase your words is as important as the words themselves. The following rhetorical hints may improve your presentation:

- Repetition of the first word in several sentences: "Economical in structure. Economical in circulation. Economical in energy use."
- Repeating a slogan throughout a presentation: "The Modern Movement is dead," used again and again.
- Repeating the last word in a phrase: "So we define space, mold space, light space, and shelter space."
- Repeating the beginning and end of each sentence: "Which one cost the least? This one. Which ones provides the most? This one."
- Opening one sentence with the last word of the previous sentence: "We search for space. Space and light."
- Using a chain of duplications: "We translated functional needs into space, space into light, and light into meaning."
- Using words with double meanings: "At the heart of every project is the heart of a client."
- Rhythmically using verbs of the same person and tense: "Those who dare, succeed."
- Repeating words of like meaning: "A rising, towering, soaring monument."
- Comparing using *like* or *as:* "A foundation like a tree."
- Personifying an object: "This drainage has carved an ugly scar on the face of your property."
- Juxtaposing ideas or words: "That approach promised much but led to frustration."
- Accepting, with qualifications: "Yes, it is costly. But it's costly only over the short term."
- Apparently accepting but actually rejecting: "Yes, it is common practice. Common to buildings that collapse."
- Anticipating refutation: "Critics will call it radical. Innovative form usually results from the use of new materials."
- Asking and answering a question at the same time: "Do we hope for an excellent design? Of course."
- Pretending perplexity or inadequacy: "Of course that's beyond my experience, but it seems to me that . . ."
- Using one or a few words that mean a lot while saying little. "Perhaps."
- Presenting an idea from many viewpoints: "The design is a costly one. It is an elegant one. It's an unusual one."
- Threatening, with alternatives: "Reinforce this joint, or we'll have to take turns holding it up."
- Leaving a statement incomplete, so the audience finishes it: "So the only course of action left to us is . . ."

A Little Show Biz

If you find powerful words awkward, adding drama is going to be a lot more difficult, but bear with me.

Drama has a tradition almost as old as architecture. If we can find the similarities between a performance and a presentation, we can tap some of that tradition. The room in which you make your presentation could be thought of as a stage with an audience. You have a cast in your design team. The pursuit of design excellence is a worthy plot, with all the elements of conflict, suspense, variety, emotion, and life. It has real, living heros and heroines that are habitually concealed from clients. The lines are right there in the presentation outline. A designer's movements about the room from model to charts to the slide screen can be choreographed.

Still a little too flamboyant? All right, but at least investigate the dramatic potential offered by inexpensive special lighting effects.

A little show biz can attract attention, favorable if handled correctly. It can emphasize your design's features, heighten positive emotions, and create action. But show biz cannot add even one gram to the value of the design solution.

Look within your solution for the real-life drama that is there. Never add unrelated entertainment, which will only distract the client from the real issues. Instead, dramatize the main issue to make it more profound, understandable, human, and compelling.

ETHICS**10**

Architects must gain their client's full approval, but they have always had serious reservations about "selling" their work. Although cautious interest in increased persuasive ability is occasionally voiced, the ethical dangers have often outweighed the potential usefulness of employing conventional sales techniques. At points this book has ventured into this forbidden area. Powerful tools of persuasion open the profession to abuses. It would be irresponsible to introduce the tools and ignore the ethical implications that are raised.

Persuasion is not evil in itself. Often it is unethical not to persuade others. The architect carries many responsibilities in serving his client, the public, and the profession. Responsibilities such as public safety cannot be forfeited in the face of powerful and diverse opposition. Salemanship may become a necessary tool in being able to fulfill these responsibilities while retaining support for the project. However, these same tools can become unethical in three ways: motive, method, and results.

Motive: If the welfare of the client, the building's users, the public, or the profession demands that an architect persuade others no evil is done, then the motive is correct and persuasion can be used. Motives beyond these should be avoided.

Method: Even in the pursuit of an ethical motive, unethical means are not justified. However useful, no technique in this book should be used in a manner that might lead to the following abuses.

In the heat of persuasion a small inaccuracy or misunderstanding could seem insignificant. Subtle misrepresentation is possible for a skillful salesman. It can be accomplished by subtle shifts of emphasis, misleading inferences, or even silence. In the vigorous interaction within a vital market-place, it can even be unintentional. Whatever the cause, the result would be unacceptable to an architect. The client would not have had free choice based on the real facts. A fact, incidentally, dwells in the past. It has happened and is therefore known to be so. The future is less certain. In a presentation, it would be inappropriate to confuse beliefs and hopes with facts.

Sales personnel have infectious personalities. It is right that a client likes the architect that serves him. Of course, this cannot be allowed to become the basis for approving a design. At times the client may lack sufficient background to make a decision on a specific issue. Although time consuming, it is essential to provide all the necessary data, even that information that does not support the architect's viewpoint. Occasionally the background information is so extensive that the architect must ask the client to accept it on trust. This trust is earned by the architect's full and fair explanations in the past, not by his personality.

Emotional appeals can be part of a presentation. They are effective but ethically dangerous. If a buyer does not get emotional satisfaction, he was cheated of something important. The client deserves the pride, anticipation, and excitement of a project, but this cannot be used to resolve a design shortcoming.

Many employees that are involved in preparing a presentation will not actually face the client. This anonymity does not eliminate the need for ethical execution. Exaggerated perspectives from impossible viewpoints, entourage that covers design weaknesses, and manipulation of scales on statistical tables are examples of abuses to be avoided.

Results: Successful designs evolve among thinking people. The concerns of clients, consultants, contractors, and employees are necessary to develop a shared knowledge that is greater than the problem that is faced. Competitive ideas are proposed and defended during this process. This competition encourages diversity of approach, improves services, and identifies flaws in the final design. Criticism is necessary and useful. Therefore, it can be ethically dangerous to become too skillful at rapidly quieting criticism with sales techniques. To quiet criticism before this flow of ideas can take place would rob everyone of its many benefits.

Unfortunately, there are also risks involved in gaining the benefits of competitive ideas. Even if a wonderful building evolves, the price in human terms can be too high. The casualties of a heated negotiation or the embarrassment of a colleague is an excessive price to pay even for a wonderful building.

In closing the best single guidance is that the package should not be better than its contents. A presentation should not be better than the design.

DRAWING AND RENDERING SAMPLES

11

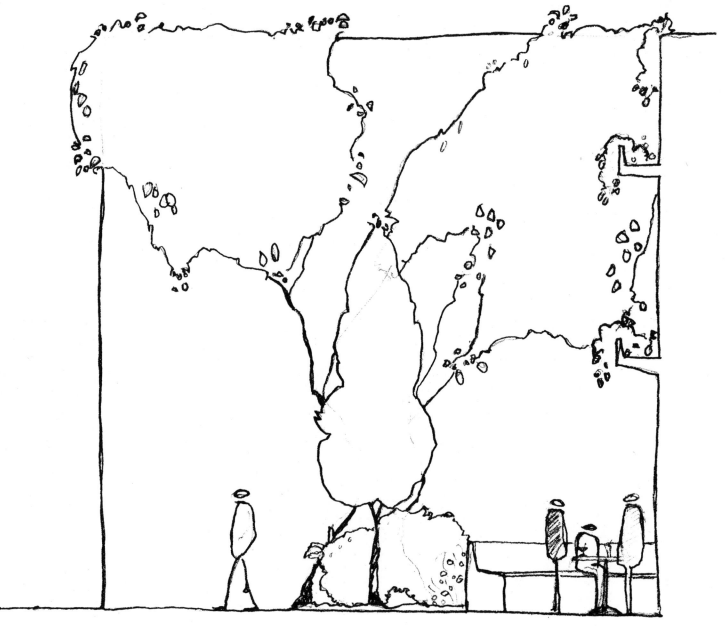

11-1. Student project by Mark Flansburg, University of Oklahoma: proposed courtyard, early conceptual sketch. Graphite pencil, 8½- by 11-inch tracing paper.

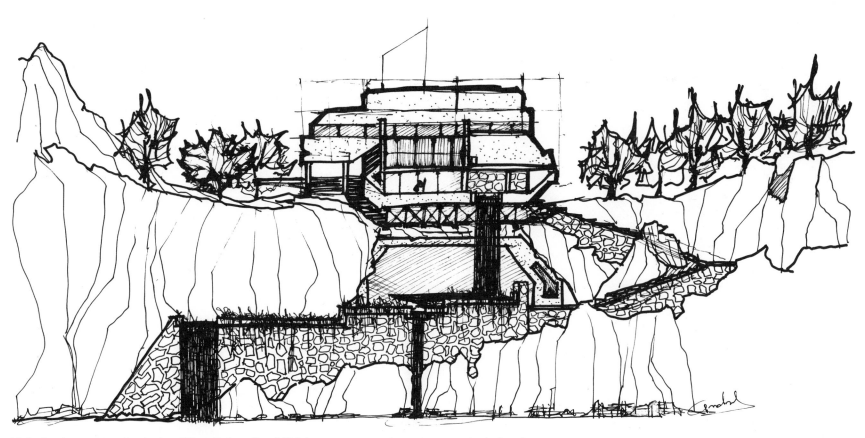

11-2. Student project by Andres Elias, University of Oklahoma: proposed resort, conceptual elevation. Razor-point and Flair pens, 10- by 16-inch tracing paper.

11-3. Student project by Pat Schoenfeldt, University of Oklahoma: proposed planting plan, conceptual drawing. Graphite pencil, 11- by 11-inch vellum.

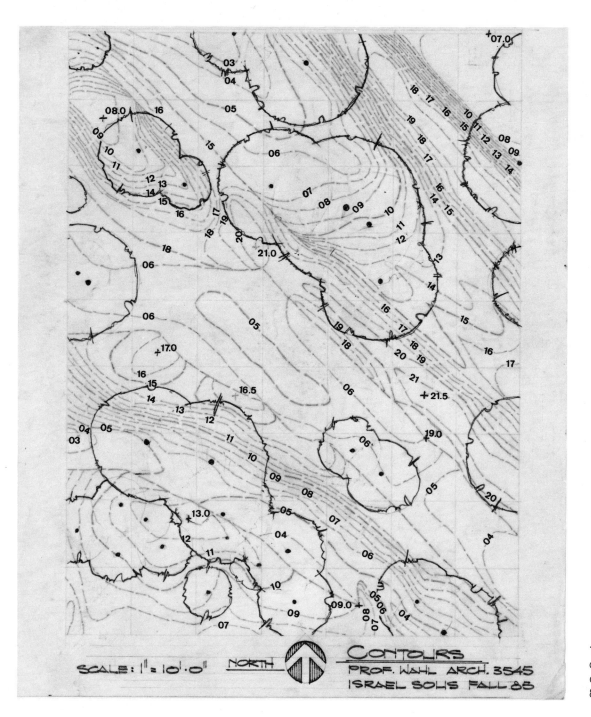

11-4. Student project by Israel Solis, University of Oklahoma: topographic contour study, conceptual plan. Graphite pencil on both sides of 8½- by 11-inch vellum.

11-5. Student project by Sharon Rissling, University of Oklahoma: proposed entry route for Bethel Baptist Church, Norman, OK, conceptual perspective. Graphite pencil, 18- by 24-inch tracing paper.

11-6. Student project by Steve Prusinskas, University of Oklahoma: proposed residence, presentation perspective. Blueline print of graphite pencil, 24- by 36-inch vellum.

11-7. Student project by Keith Iott, University of
Oklahoma: London Program Sketches:
presentation perspective. Graphite pencil, 18- by
24-inch Strathmore paper.

11-8. Student project by Keith Iott, University of Oklahoma: Soho design, presentation perspective. Graphite pencil, 18- by 24-inch Strathmore paper.

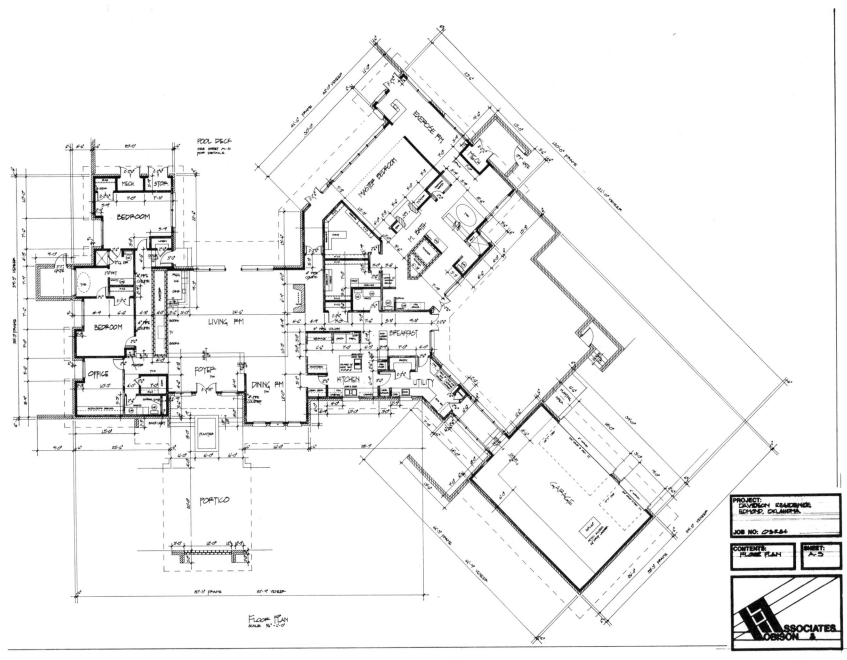

11-9. Mark Robison, Robison Associates: Davidson residence, Edmond, OK, mechanical plan.
Technical pencil, 24- by 36-inch Mylar.

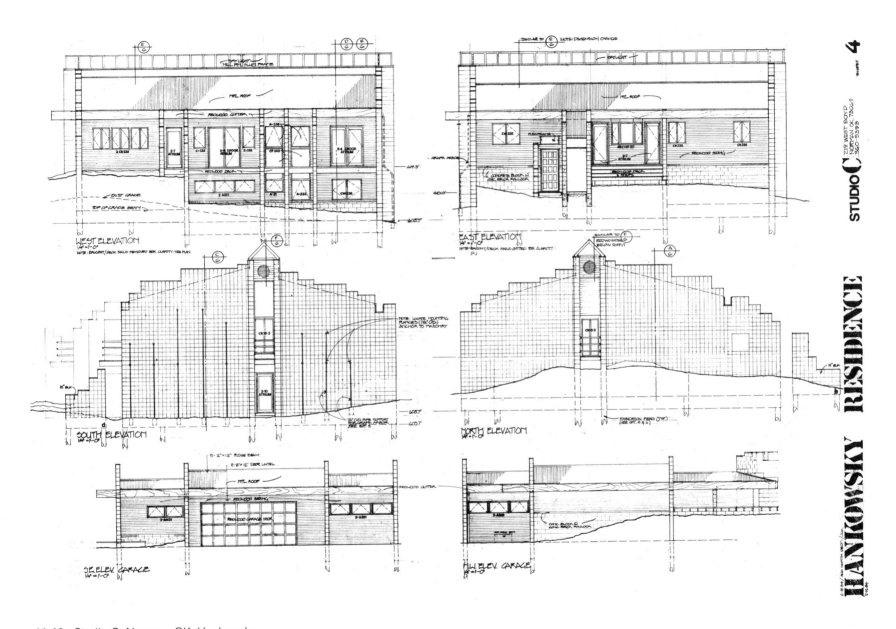

STUDIO C
219 WEST BOYD
NORMAN OK 73069
360-5393

WEST ELEVATION
1/4" = 1'-0"
NOTE: BALCONY/DECK RAILS REMOVED FOR CLARITY-SEE PLAN

EAST ELEVATION
1/4" = 1'-0"
NOTE: BALCONY/DECK RAILS OMITTED FOR CLARITY.

SOUTH ELEVATION
1/4" = 1'-0"

NORTH ELEVATION
1/4" = 1'-0"

SE ELEV. GARAGE
1/4" = 1'-0"

NW ELEV. GARAGE
1/4" = 1'-0"

HANKOWSKY RESIDENCE

11-10. Studio C, Norman, OK: Hankowsky
residence, Norman, OK, working drawings.
Graphite pencil, 24- by 36-inch vellum.

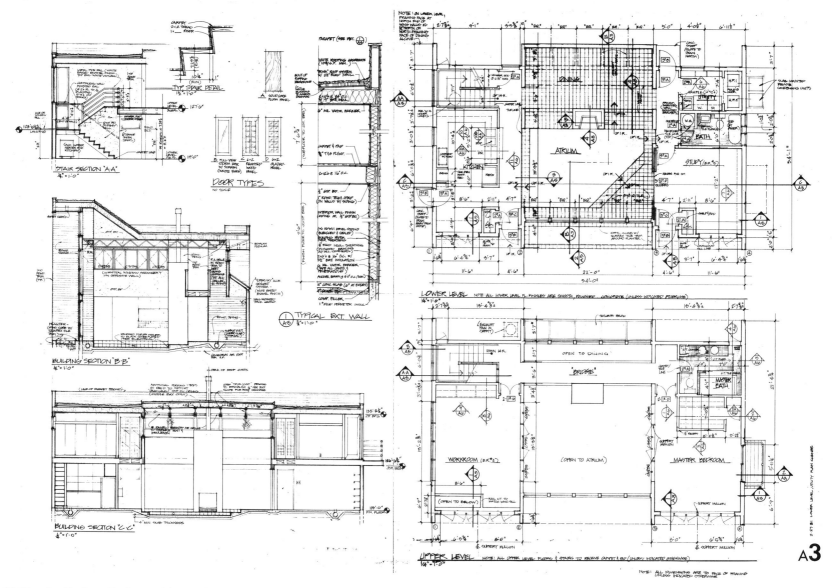

11-11. Jim Kudrna: Enrico residence, Lake Eufaula, OK, working drawings. Graphite pencil, 24- by 36-inch vellum.

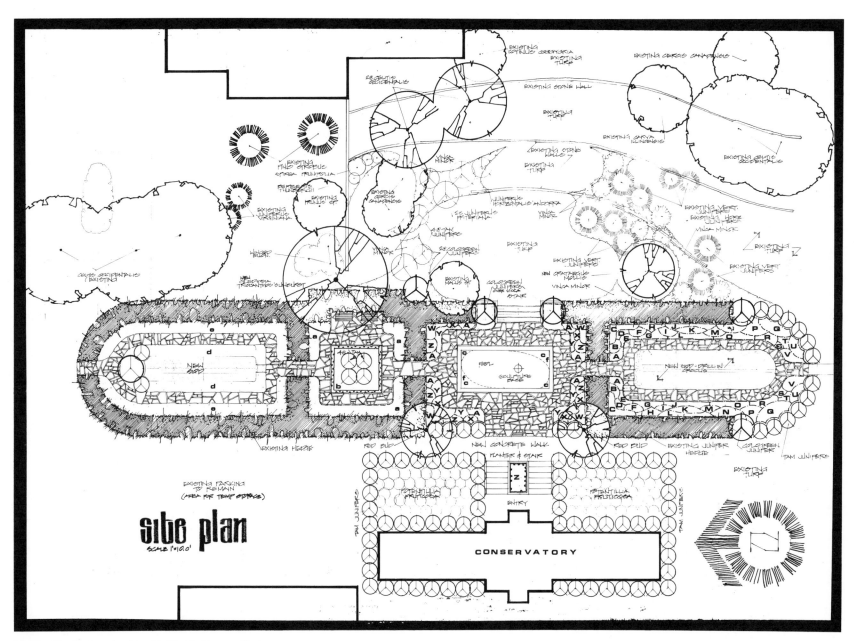

11-12. Student project by M. Wahl, Kansas State University: proposed formal garden renovation, presentation plan. Graphite pencil and ink, 24- by 36-inch vellum.

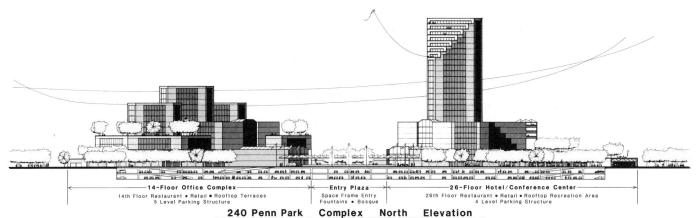

14-Floor Office Complex
14th Floor Restaurant • Retail • Rooftop Terraces
5 Level Parking Structure

Entry Plaza
Space Frame Entry
Fountains • Bosque

26-Floor Hotel/Conference Center
26th Floor Restaurant • Retail • Rooftop Recreation Area
4 Level Parking Structure

240 Penn Park   Complex   North   Elevation

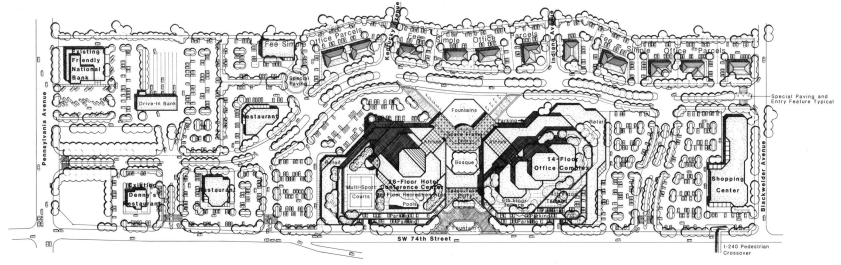

Development Plan Statistics

	Gross Floor Area	Required Parking
Hotel/Conference Center	471,410	1,223
Hotel-500 rms. 302,500		
Conference Center 77,300		
Retail 85,910		
Restaurant 5,700		
Office Complex	443,250	1,429
Offices 404,500		
Retail 29,550		
Restaurant 9,200		

	Gross Floor Area	Required Parking
Fee Simple Office Parcels	88,600	
Shopping Center	34,500	185
Retail 30,000		
Restaurant(s) 4,500		
Restaurants	18,000	
Total New Development	1,055,760	

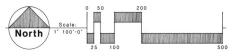

North

Scale:
1' 100'-0"

0 50   200
25 100   500

environmetrics
urban design   land planning   landscape architecture
oklahoma city, oklahoma   405-751-0445

DATE: 10/8/84   REVISED:

240 PENN PARK

A   P. B. Odom III   Development
Oklahoma City,   Oklahoma

Plaza Shops and Offices   Dock at Lake Front Plaza   Restaurant and/or Theater

Town Center

11-14. Dan Lare, ASLA, Environmetrics: Boyles
Landing, Lawton, OK, presentation elevations.
Razor-point and Flair pens, 12- by 24-inch tracing
paper.

11-13. *(facing page)* Michael Parks,
Environmetrics: 240 Penn Park, Oklahoma City,
OK, presentation drawings. Technical pen and
Zipatone pattern screen, 24- by 36-inch vellum.

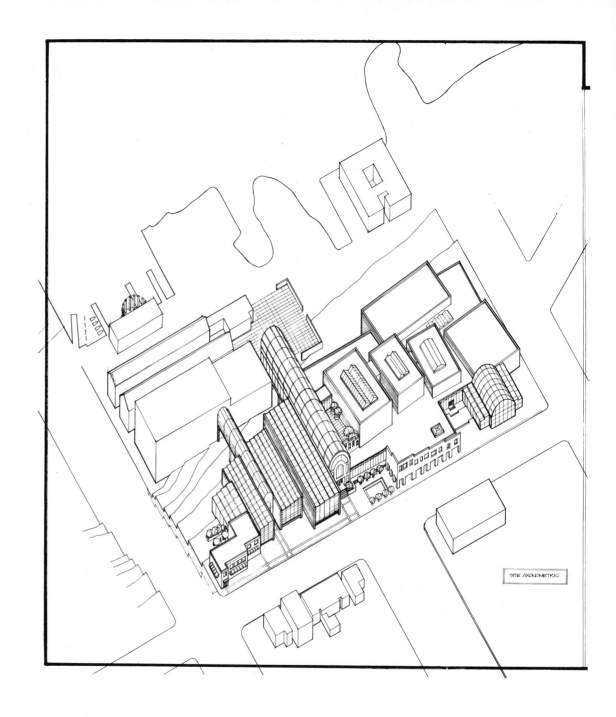

SITE AXONOMETRIC

11-15. Student project by Audrey McClurg,
University of Oklahoma: site axonometric.
Technical pencil, 24- by 24-inch Mylar.

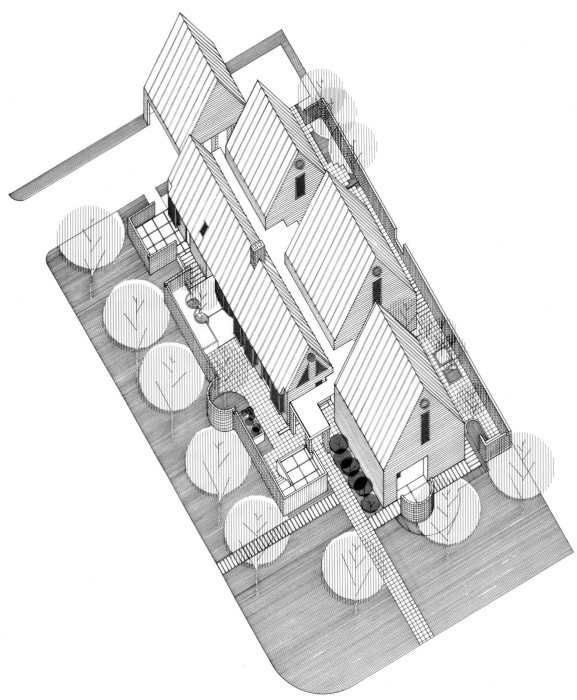

11-16. Studio C—Nick Harm, drawing; Ron Hess, design: proposed rectory, St. Thomas More Church, Norman, OK, presentation isometric. Technical pen and Zipatone pattern screen, 18-by 24-inch vellum.

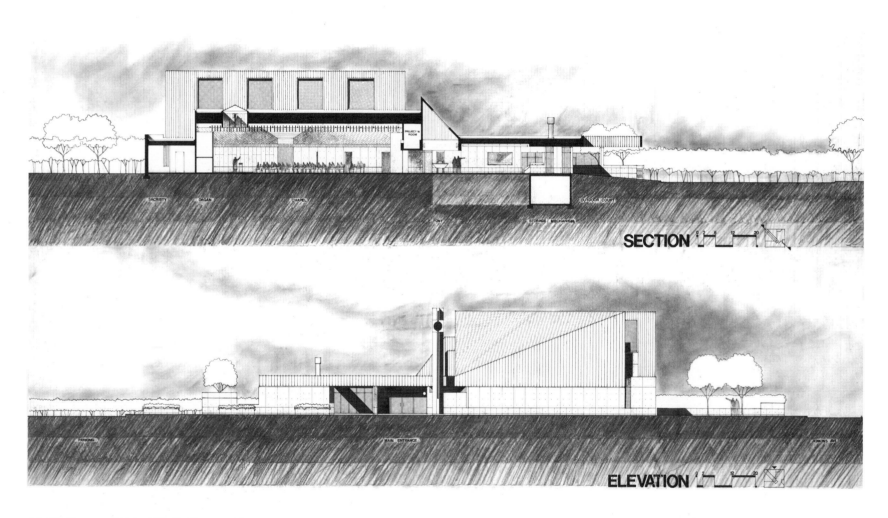

11-17. Raymond Yeh, AIA: St. Thomas More
Church, Norman, OK, presentation drawings
(Award of Excellence, Oklahoma chapter AIA).
Graphite pencil and Zipatone pattern screen. 24-
by 26-inch vellum.

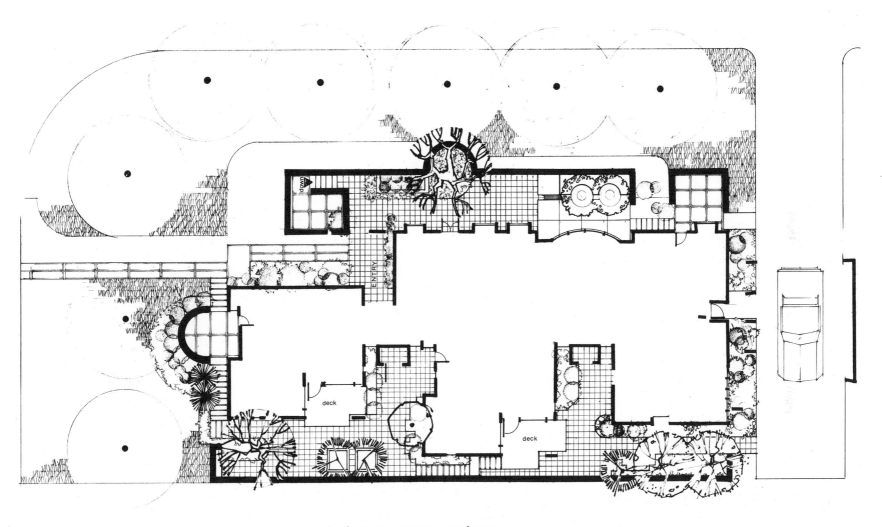

st. thomas more rectory
norman, oklahoma

11-18. M. Wahl, Studio C: St. Thomas More
Church, Norman, OK, proposed rectory site plan.
Mixed media, 12- by 24-inch vellum.

University of San Diego

Terrace & Plaza

11-19. Jim Kudrna, drawing; James Yock, design: proposed terrace and plaza, University of San Diego, presentation perspective. Technical pens, 24- by 36-inch Mylar.

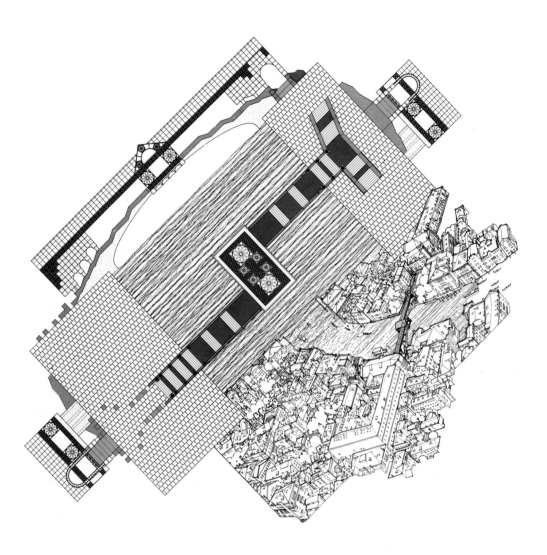

11-20. Brad Black, Bob Hogan, Jim Kudrna, and Ron Hess: Ponte del'Accademia, presentation drawing (Venice Biennale competition entry). Computer and ink line, 52- by 52-inch vellum.

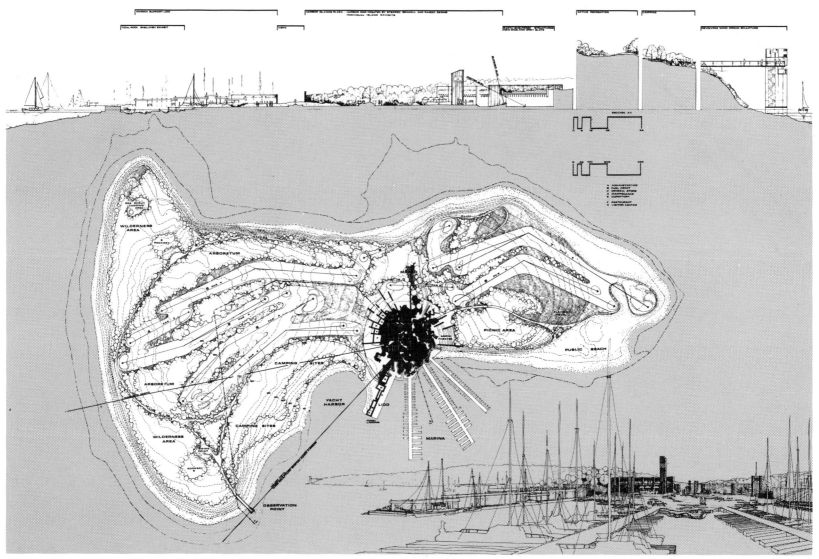

S·P·E·C·T·A·C·L·E I·S·L·A·N·D
BOSTON HARBOR STATE PARK
R·E·C·R·E·A·T·I·O·N C·E·N·T·R·E

11-21. Nick Harm, Jim Kudrna, and Iver Wahl: Spectacle Island, Boston harbor, presentation drawing (competition entry). Ink and layered negative, 30- by 40-inch Mylar.

11-22. Dan Lare, ASLA, Environmetrics: Harpoon Louie's, Jupiter, FL, presentation perspective. Colored markers, 24- by 36-inch Diazoprint.

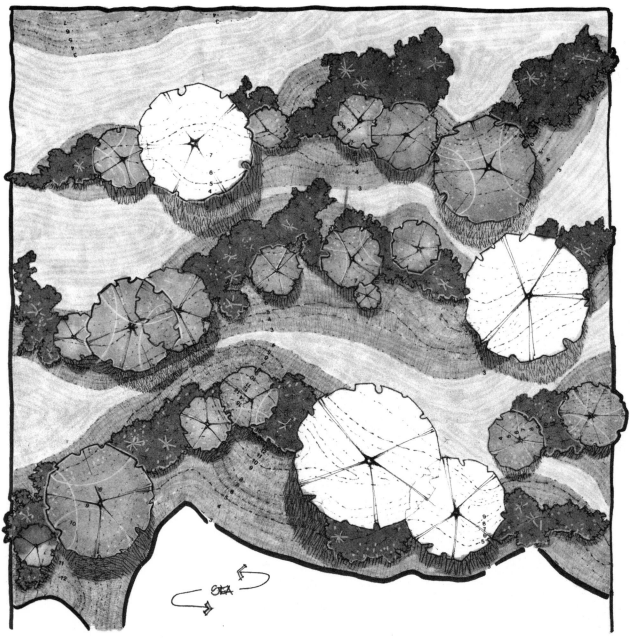

11-23. Student project by Amy J. G. Lim,
University of Oklahoma: site design, presentation
plan. Colored markers, 14- by 14-inch Diazoprint.

AMY J. G. LIM

126 DRAWING AND RENDERING SAMPLES

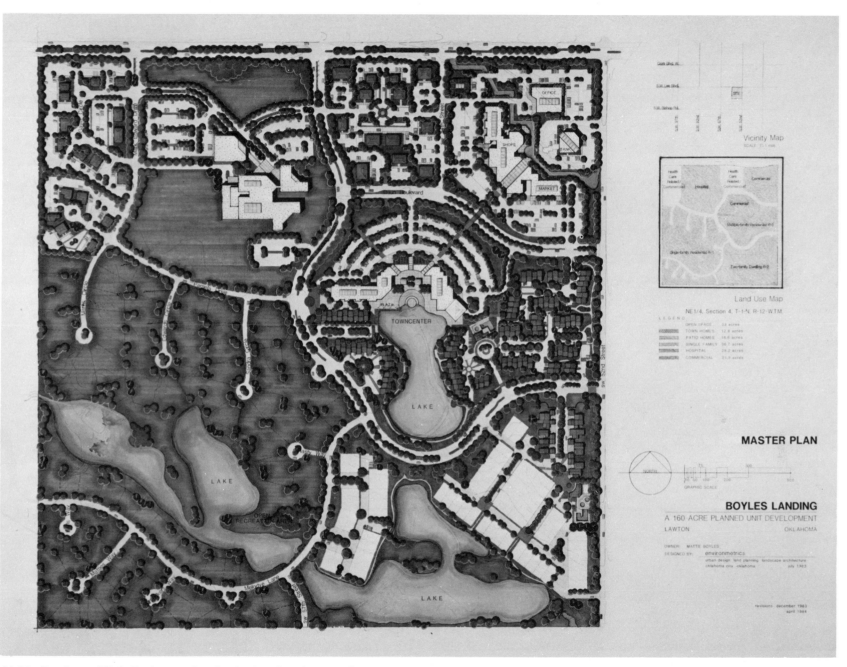

11-24. Dan Lare, ASLA, Environmetrics: Boyles Landing, Lawton, OK, presentation plan. Colored markers, 24- by 36-inch Diazoprint.

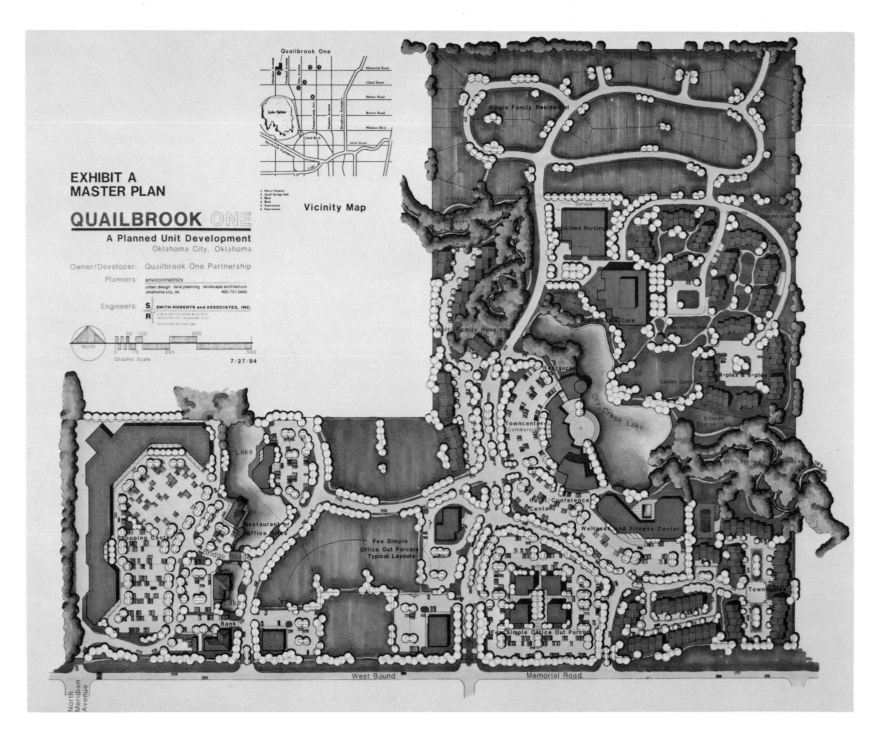

11-25. *(facing page)* Dan Lare, ASLA, Environmetrics: Quailbrook, Oklahoma City, OK, presentation plan. Colored markers, 24- by 36-inch Diazoprint.

11-26. Student project by Rob Yacobian, University of Oklahoma: multiuse high-rise, presentation perspective. Watercolor and airbrush, 18- by 24-inch Strathmore paper.

BIBLIOGRAPHY

American Institute of Architects. *Architect's Handbook of Professional Practice*. Washington, DC: American Institute of Architects, 1969.

Arnett, William E. *Santayana and the Sense of Beauty*. Bloomington, IN: Indiana University Press, 1957.

Ashwin, Clive. *Encyclopedia of Drawing*. Cincinnati: North Light Publishers, 1982.

Association of General Contractors. *CPM in Construction*. Washington, DC: Associated General Contractors of America, 1965.

Bernard, Frank J. *Dynamic Display*. Cincinnati, OH: The Display Publishing Co., 1962.

Braun, Paul G. *Figure Composition*. New York: Bridgman Publications, Inc., 1930.

Bro, Lu. *Drawing: A Studio Guide*. New York: W.W. Norton and Co., 1979.

Burden, Earnest. *Entourage: A Tracing File for Architecture and Interior Design Drawing*. New York: McGraw-Hill Book Co., 1981.

Butler, Ralph Starr. "What the Advertiser Owes the Public." In *Ethical Problems of Modern Advertising* by William A. Vawter Foundation. New York: The Roland Press Co., 1931.

Camp, Jeffery. *The Drawing Book*. New York: Holt, Reinhart, and Winston, 1981.

Chase, Stuart. "The Ethics of Advertising as Viewed by the Consumer." In *Ethical Problems of Modern Advertising* by William A. Vawter Foundation. New York: The Roland Press Co., 1931.

Chermayeff, Serge, and Christopher Alexander. *Community and Privacy: Toward a New Architecture of Humanism*. New York: Doubleday and Co., Inc., 1963.

Cohen, Herb. *You Can Negotiate Anything*. New York: Bantam Books, 1982.

Cooper, Joseph D. *Handbook for Sales Meetings, Conventions, and Conferences*. New London, CT: National Sales Development Institute, 1959.

Coulin, Claudius. *Step-by-Step Perspective Drawing*. Rev. ed. New York: Van Nostrand Reinhold Co., 1984.

Croce, Benedetto. *Aesthetic*. Douglas Ainslie, trans. New York: Godine, 1978.

Cullen, Gordon. *The Concise Townscape*. New York: Van Nostrand Reinhold Co., 1961.

Descarques, Pierre. *Perspective: History, Evolution, and Techniques*. I. M. Paris, trans. New York: Van Nostrand Reinhold Co., 1982.

Dessoir, Max. *Aesthetics and Theory of Art*. Stephen A. Emery, trans. Detroit: Wayne State University Press, 1970.

Dondis, Donis A. *A Primer of Visual Literacy*. Cambridge, MA: MIT Press, 1973.

Doyle, Michael E. *Color Drawing: A Marker—Colored-Pencil Approach*. New York: Van Nostrand Reinhold Co., 1981.

Duncan, Robert. *Architectural Graphics and Communication*. Dubuque, IO: Kendall/Hunt Publishing Co., 1980.

Evans, Larry. *Illustration Guide for Architects, De-signers and Students*. New York: Van Nostrand Reinhold Co., 1982.

Fast, Julius. *Body Language*. New York: Simon and Schuster, Pocket Books, 1984.

Forseth, Kevin, with David Vaughan. *Graphics for Architecture*. New York: Van Nostrand Reinhold Co., 1979.

Gardner, James, and Caroline Heller. *Exhibition and Display*. London: B.T. Batsford, Ltd., 1960.

Goodban, William T., and Jack J. Hayslett. *Architectural Drawing and Planning*. New York: McGraw-Hill Book Co., 1979.

Goode, Kenneth M., and M. Zenn Kaufman. *Showmanship in Business*. New York: Harper and Brothers, 1936.

Griffin, C.W. *Development Building: The Team Approach*. New York: John Wiley and Sons, Halstead Press, 1972.

Halse, Albert O. *Architectural Rendering: The Technique of Contemporary Presentation*. 2nd ed. New York: McGraw-Hill Book Co., 1972.

Hattwick, Melvin S. *How to Use Psychology for Better Advertising*. Englewood Cliffs, NJ: Prentice-Hall, Inc., 1950.

Hohauser, Sanford, with Helen Demchyshyn. *Architectural and Interior Models: Design and Construction*. 2nd ed. New York: Van Nostrand Reinhold Co., 1984.

Horvath, Walter. *Miracle Sales Guide*. Englewood Cliffs, NJ: Prentice-Hall, Inc., 1962.

Husband, Richard W. *The Psychology of Success-*

ful Selling. New York: Harper and Brothers, 1953.

Jacoby, Helmut. *Architectural Drawings*. New York: Architectural Book Publishing Co., Inc., 1977.

Kautzky, Ted. *The Ted Kautzky Pencil Book*. New York: Van Nostrand Reinhold Co., 1979.

Kemmerich, Carl. *Graphic Details for Architects*. New York: Frederick A. Praeger, 1968.

Korda, Michael. *Power: How to Get It, How to Use It*. New York: Random House, Ballantine Books, 1976.

Lao Tsu. *Tao Teh Ching*. Gia-Fu Feng, ed. Jane English, trans. New York: Random House/Vintage, 1972.

Letterman, Elmer G. *The Sale Begins When the Customer Says No*. New York: Greenberg Publishers, 1953.

Lin, Mike W. *Architectural Rendering Techniques: A Color Reference*. New York: Van Nostrand Reinhold Co., 1985.

Lockard, William Kirby. *Design Drawing Experiences*. 4th ed. Tucson: Pepper Publishing Co., 1979.

————. *Drawing as a Means to Architecture*. Tucson: Pepper Publishing Co., 1977.

Marshall, Lane L. *Landscape Architecture: Guidelines to Professional Practice*. Washington, DC: American Society of Landscape Architects, 1981.

Mauger, Emily M. *Modern Display Techniques*. New York: Fairchild Publications, Inc., 1964.

McHugh, Robert C. *Working Drawing Handbook*. New York: Van Nostrand Reinhold Co., 1977.

Morang, Alfred. *Adventures in Drawing*. Denver: Sage Books, Inc., 1947.

Munce, Howard, and Robert Fawcett. *Drawing the Nude*. New York: Watson-Guptill Publications, 1980.

Nicolaides, Kimon. *The Natural Way to Draw*. Boston: Houghton Mifflin Co., 1941.

Nierenberg, Gerard I., and Henry H. Calero. *How to Read a Person Like a Book*. New York: Simon and Schuster, Cornerstone, 1972.

Olgay, Victor. *Design with Climate*. Princeton, NJ: Princeton University Press, 1963.

Oliver, Robert S. *The Sketch*. New York: Van Nostrand Reinhold Co., 1979.

Omang, Joanne. *Psychological Operations in Guerrilla Warfare*. New York: Random House/Vintage, 1985.

Parker, DeWitt H. *The Principles of Aesthetics*. 2nd ed. 1946. Reprint. Westport, CT: Greenwood Press, 1976.

Porter, Tom, and Bob Greenstreet. *Manual of Graphic Techniques*. New York: Charles Scribner's Sons, 1980.

Prall, D. *Aesthetic Judgment*. New York: Thomas Y. Crowell Co., 1967.

Ramsey, Charles G., and Harold R. Sleeper. *Architectural Graphic Standards*. 6th ed. New York: John Wiley and Sons, Inc., 1970.

Reid, Louis Arnaud. *A Study in Aesthetics*. Westport, CT: Greenwood Press, 1973.

Rowe, Frank A. *Display Fundamentals*. Cincinnati: The Display Publishing Co., 1965.

Rubenstein, Harvey M. *A Guide to Site and Environmental Planning*. New York: John Wiley and Sons, Inc., 1980.

Russell, Frederic A., Frank H. Beach, and Richard H. Buskirk. *Textbook of Salesmanship*. New York: McGraw-Hill Book Co., Inc, 1963.

Simonds, John Ormsbee. *Landscape Architecture: A Manual of Site Planning and Design*. New York: McGraw-Hill Book Co., Inc., 1983.

Staub, Calvin C. *Design Process and Communications*. Dubuque, IO: Kendall/Hunt Publishing Co., 1978.

Szabo, Marc. *Drawing File for Architects, Illustrators, and Designers*. New York: Van Nostrand Reinhold Co., 1976.

Thayer, Lee O. *Sales and Engineering Representation*. New York: McGraw-Hill Book Co., 1958.

Thomas, Marvin L. *Architectural Working Drawings*. New York: McGraw-Hill Book Co., 1978.

Turner, James R. *Drawing with Confidence: A Manual for Architects, Landscape Architects, and Artists*. New York: Van Nostrand Reinhold Co., 1984.

VanDyke, Scott. *From Line to Design: Design Graphics Communication*. West Lafayette, IN: PDA Publishing Corp., 1982.

Wales, Hugh G., Dwight L. Gentry, and Max Wales. *Advertising, Copy, Layout, and Typography*. New York: The Roland Press Co., 1958.

Wang, Thomas C. *Plan and Section Drawing*. New York: Van Nostrand Reinhold Co., 1979.

Weld, L.D.H. "Honesty in Fact Finding." In *Ethical Problems of Modern Advertising* by William A. Vawter Foundation. New York: The Roland Press Co., 1931.

White, Edward T. *A Graphic Vocabulary for Architectural Presentation*. Tucson: Architectural Media, Ltd. 1972.

Whiteside, Robert L. *Face Language*. New York: Simon and Schuster, Pocket Books, 1984.

Whittier, Charles L. *Creative Advertising*. New York: Holt, Rinehart, and Winston, Inc., 1955.

Wright, John S., and Daniel S. Warner. *Advertising*. New York: McGraw-Hill Book Co., Inc., 1962.

INDEX

abstraction, 13
adequacy, of composition, 30
adhesive shading films, 80
airbrush, 78
Alberti, Leon Battista, 30
Architectural Graphics and Communications (Duncan), 59
Architectural Graphic Standards (Ramsey and Sleeper), 70
Architectural Rendering (Halse), 70, 78
associative content, 30
asymmetry, 36
automobiles, 68
axial organization, 37
axonometric drawings, 46

balance, 36
body language, 4, 95
Building Construction Illustrated (Ching), 70

Carnegie, Dale, 31
Ching, Frank, 70
chroma, 35, 43
circular organization, 37
clarity, 30
clients. *See also* Presentations
    appeals to, 2
    approval from, 97
    attitudes of, 2
    and design content, 31
    information about, 2
    instincts of, 2
    interpretation by, 31–32
    learned behavior of, 2
    motives of, 2
    negative responses from, 3–4
    objections by, 96–97

positive responses from, 3
    selling to, 94
color, 34–35, 41–43
Color Drawing (Doyle), 77
colored pencil, 74, 77
color temperature, 35
compensation, 3
composite graphic analyses, 22
composition
    elements of content for, 32–36
    elements of order in, 36
    goals of, 30
    principles of, 30
    steps in, 38–43
    systems of order in, 37
    theory of, 30–32
conceptual drawings, 17, 24, 25
construction materials, 70–72
content, 30–31, 38
contour line drawing, 10, 74
Coulin, Claudius, 59
counterpoint, 32
critical edges, 33
cubist drawing, 9

Design Drawing Experiences (Lockard), 66
design phases
    analysis, 22
    organization, 20–21
    research, 21–22
    synthesis, 24–25
dominance, 36
Dondis, Donis, 32
Doyle, Michael, 77
drawing. *See also* Composition; Entourage; Graphic languages; Projections
    abstraction, 13
    contour line, 10

cubist, 9
    gesture, 6–7
    life, 12
    memory, 11
    minimal, 10
    photo, 11
    proportional, 7–8
    scumbling, 7
    serial sketches, 13
    structural, 9
    thumbnail sketches, 12
    tools and equipment for, 6
    window, 9
Duncan, Robert, 59

emphasis, 30
entourage, 43
    drawing, 62–63
    elegant figures, 64
    furniture, 69–70
    plant materials, 65
    vehicles, 68
escape mechanisms, 3–4
ethics, 102
exhibits
    planning, 92
    principles of, 90–91
    vocabulary of, 92

flow charts, 20–21
focal point, 32
form, 33
formal balance, 36
furniture, 69–70

geometric organization, 37
geometric shape, 33
gesture drawing, 6–7

grain, 34
Graphic Details for Architects (Kemmerich), 65
graphic languages
  conceptual, 17
  mechanical, 18
  schematic, 16
Graphic Vocabulary for Architectural Presentation, A, (White), 70
ground covers, 66

Halse, Albert, 70, 78
harmony, 30
Hohauser, Sanford, 88
houseplants, 66
hue, 34–35, 41–43

ideas, 30
identification, 4
implied line, 33
informal balance, 36
ink, 77

Jacoby, Helmut, 77

Kautsky, Theodore, 70, 74
Kemmerich, Carl, 65, 66

lettering, 13–14, 80
life drawing, 12
light, 34, 40–41
Lin, Mike, 78
line, 32–33, 39–40
Lockard, William Kirby, 66, 77

markers, 74, 77–78
mass, 34
mechanical drawing, 18, 25
media
  airbrush, 78
  choosing, 31, 39
  colored pencil, 77
  felt-tip markers, 77–78
  graphite pencil, 74
  pastels, 78
  pen-and-ink, 77
  watercolor, 78
memory drawing, 11
minimal drawing, 10
models, 80–87

objective content, 30–31
oblique drawings, 46
Oliver, Robert, 64
orthographic drawings, 46
outline, 33

paper, 6
paraline projections, 46
pastels, 78
pattern, 34, 37
pencil, 74
Pencil Broadsides (Kautsky), 70
pens, 6, 77
people, 62–64
personnel charts, 21
perspective projections
  freehand, 47, 48–49
  mechanical, 47, 50–59
photo drawing, 11
pie graphs, 21
Plan and Section Drawing (Wang), 65
planes, 33, 40
points, 32, 39
presentations
  conclusions of, 97
  exciting interest during, 96
  gaining approval in, 97
  goals of, 94
  holding attention during, 96
  introduction to, 95
  objections during, 96–97
  planning, 94–95
  questions during, 96
  rehearsing, 95
  rhetoric for, 98
  selling in, 94
  theatrics in, 98–99
  tools for, 97–98
Primer for Visual Literacy, A, (Dondis), 32
projections, 38
  paraline, 46
  perspective, 46, 47–59
proportion, 36
proportional drawing, 7–8
proximity, 36

Ramsey, Charles, 70
rationalization, 4
reflective materials, 71–72
regression, 3–4

Reid, Louis Arnaud, 30
repetition, 36
repression, 4
rhythm, 37

scale, 36
schematic language, 16, 20–24
scumbling, 7
sequence, 36
serial sketches, 13
shades, 35
shape, 33–34, 40
shrubs, 66
silhouette, 33
similarity, 36
simplicity, 30
Sketch, The, (Oliver), 64
Sleeper, Harold, 70
space, 32
Step-by-Step Perspective Drawing (Coulin), 59
straight line, 33
structural drawing, 9
structure, 31
Study in Aesthetics, A, (Reid), 30
subjective content, 30
sublimation, 3–4
suitability, of composition, 30
symmetry, 36

texture, 34, 40
theme, 37
thumbnail sketches, 12
tint, 35
tone, 35
tracing files, 72
trees, 65
trends, 37
triangular organization, 37

undulation, 37
unity, in composition, 30

value, 35, 43
variety, in composition, 30
visual aids, for presentations, 97
volume, 34

Wang, Thomas, 65, 66, 77
watercolor, 78
White, Edward, 70
window drawing, 9